PLANTS OF MYSTERY AND MAGIC

PLANTS OF MYSTERY AND MAGIC

A PHOTOGRAPHIC GUIDE

MICHAEL JORDAN

BLANDFORD

A BLANDFORD BOOK

First published in the UK 1997 by Blandford

A Cassell Imprint
Cassell Plc, Wellington House,
125 Strand, London WC2R OBB

Distributed in the United States by Sterling Publishing Co., Inc.,
387 Park Avenue South, New York, NY 10016-8810

British Library Cataloguing-in-Publication Data
A catalogue entry for this title is available from the British Library

ISBN 0-7137-2645-8

Photograph of *Boletus satanas* (p.111) courtesy of David Lester.
Photograph of *Quercus* (Spp.) (pp.77, 100) courtesy of Betty Jordan.

Cover Design: Jamie Tanner
Design: Richard Carr

Printed and bound in Hong Kong by Colorcraft Ltd

Contents

PART ONE

Herbaceous Plants and Shrubs 7

PART TWO

Trees 77

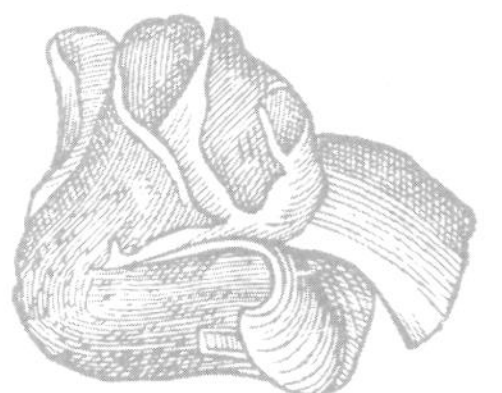

PART THREE

Fungi 107

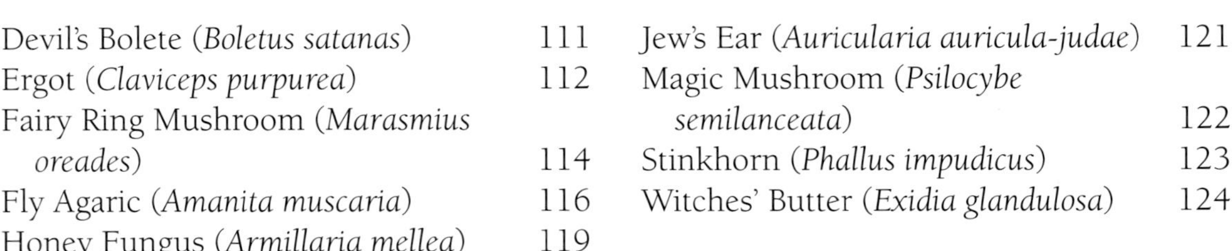

PART ONE

Herbaceous Plants and Shrubs

PART ONE

Herbaceous Plants and Shrubs

Introduction

THE FAMILY OF TREES known as *Boswellia* includes some inconspicuous-looking plants, yet a flask containing a minute amount of the extract of *Boswellia* sap, a mere 10 ml worth, currently sells for over $400. The extract possesses a fragrance which, while time-honoured, is neither particularly memorable nor is its liquid of any great practical value. Against it, though, an ounce of gold would be slightly cheaper. *Boswellia* is more or less limited in its distribution to the southern part of the Arabian peninsula. Moving into North Africa and Ethiopia, the *Commiphora* genus, another family of small subtropical trees, produces a resin which, while not having the same commercial value, has been prized since Biblical times for its mystical and pain-killing properties. So what is it that makes the extracts from these plants so noteworthy? It is an association part mystical, part magical – the sap of *Boswellia* is better known as Frankincense and the resin of the *Commiphora* trees is Myrrh.

If it is clear, from the earliest art and archaeological evidence of humankind's conscious interest in the world of nature, that animals were imbued with an aura of mystery and magic, it is also probably true that ancient man held plants in a special kind of reverence, though this is not so obvious in those vestiges of his belief which have survived the passage of time. While the arcane art galleries of the Ice Age in southwestern Europe teem with animal and human figures, there are only scant signs of flowers, leaves and twigs. Other evidence, though, suggests that there was a very keen interest in the plant world that went beyond its utilitarian value as a source of food, fuel, clothing, weapons and housing material – evidence that comes from the remains of ritual meals, from burial sites and from traditions of more modern remnants of the ancient hunting tribes.

So what special properties have given plants their particular air of mystique? Two groups of plants at opposite ends of the evolutionary chain, the trees and the fungi, have acquired particular sentient associations which are dealt with in separate sections of this book and which are, in some respects, comparatively easy to understand. The great mass of greenery in between, though, lacks the qualities of immanence that can be attached to an Oak tree or a garishly coloured, phallic-shaped mushroom, so what is it that has given herbaceous plants and shrubs the qualities of mystery and magic that are often still greatly respected at the close of the sophisticated, technological, worldly-wise twentieth century? If the notion of occult belief in weeds raises an eyebrow, consider how many of us would decline to wear a red Poppy on Remembrance Sunday or refuse a sprig of Heather from a gypsy? We scour the ground for four-leaved Clovers, consider it deeply unlucky to bring certain blooms into the house in springtime, and conventionally understand white Lilies to be a sign of death. Children tell the time by Dandelion clocks and hold Buttercups under their chins for portents of future prosperity. These are all vestiges of associations which our grandparents and great-grandparents knew and understood well but which we mostly retain only through half-remembered advice and, perhaps, instincts as old as the human race itself.

The origin of plants must have puzzled ancient people and added to the sense of mystery. We take such straightforward scientific matters as pollination and fertilization for granted, but imagine living in a world in which there is no understanding of science, no technology, no microscopes. The genesis of a plant may, under those circumstances, become something of considerable wonderment, because the act of procreation does not happen visibly as it does in the animal kingdom. The minute grains of pollen, which settle on the receptive stigma and penetrate deep into the ovary to effect a discreet and subtle union, are no more than innocent grains of dust drifting on the breeze. Yet, with each spring, new generations emerge from the seemingly dead and frozen world of winter. By what agency does this annual miracle take place?

Dandelion clocks have long been a children's favourite.

In the primitive mind the secret and magical means by which plants are inseminated to grow and take substance in the womb of the earth is the warm spring rain, the life-giving essence of the gods. If the gods are the inseminators of the soil then, logically, everything which grows from the earth is of their creation.

The early hunter-gatherers probably first took a subjective interest in plants when they discovered that certain roots and berries restored the health of a person who was ill. This curative property almost certainly had more far-reaching implications in those far-off times than it would today because of the way in which primitive tribespeople view illness and the reasons for its appearance. When the beliefs of very isolated hunting tribes in southeastern Siberia were recorded at the turn of the century, ethnologists discovered that most disease was thought of as a misfortune placed upon individuals by members of the spirit world. Within the most primitive religion of animism there is an understanding that everything in nature is controlled by one of a myriad of spirit beings, and that each personal action, whether killing an animal for food, lighting a fire, or washing up a cooking-pot, constitutes an interaction with the unseen world of spirits that exists in tandem with our own temporal frame. Any misfortune which descends on an individual member of the tribe, including illness or physical disability, is brought at the direction of the more malevolent members of the ether. Conversely, anything which relieves the symptoms of disease must be under the control of benevolent spirits.

The certainty with which primitive religion couples plants with spirit beings is revealed in many of the stories collected from the Siberian tribes before their conversion to Russian Orthodox Christianity. Their myths and legends teem with characters such as Grass Woman, Tree Trunk Man and Stone Pine Girl, who constantly drift from one state to another, one moment taking on human appearance, the next disguised in the form of the tree or the field of grass over which they stand guard as invisible entities.

The intercessors with this unseen but very pertinent world were, and, where such tribes exist, still are, the shamans, the earliest style of priests, and it was they who probably first established, by trial and error, that eating certain types of plant or drinking particular herbal juices would effect a miraculous cure.

It is impossible to establish when, in the hazy void of prehistory, these simple medical beliefs first took form, but there exists some remarkable archaeological evidence for which it is necessary to make a backward jump in time of 60,000 years. Then, Neanderthals, the forerunners of *Homo sapiens*, lived in the highlands of what is now northern Iraq. In 1960 a burial site was discovered in a remote cave near the village of Shanidar. It contained eight human skeletons, buried deep beneath the present-day cave floor. Among the remains was that of a young man who had clearly been someone of importance, since his body was circled by a ring of stones and he had been accorded special burial rites. He was laid on a bed of woody Horsetails and, over and around him (the evidence visible under a modern microscope as pollen grains amid the ancient dust of the cave) had been strewn flowers, presumably by those who interred him. There is nothing, it might be imagined, particularly remarkable in this, until one examines the qualities of the plants involved. They were identified to be Grape Hyacinths, Yellow Ragwort, Groundsel, Yarrow, Cornflower, Hollyhock and St Barnaby's Thistle. Astonishingly a modern herbal, *Materia Medica*, reveals that almost all the species are known to be remedial both in treating infected or inflamed wounds and for lowering fever. It seems that the man had been sent on a journey to another world equipped with those plants which would enable him to heal.

We have other evidence that suggests an interest in plants that went beyond more tangible effects. The Iron-Age bog corpses, so perfectly preserved in their airless and bacteria-free burial grounds, have yielded conundrums that are still unresolved. Why did the stomach of Lindow Man, from Cheshire, contain the remains of what appears to have been a ritual meal eaten immediately before he was slaughtered? Was it purely a last request or did he consume plants which were known to possess magical significance? We may never know, but the food included remnants of Mistletoe, recognized by the Druids as a plant of great sacred significance.

The study of herbs was an important facet of life in many parts of the ancient world. In Egypt, herbalists were well versed in the selective use of plants for remedial purposes, as the Eber medical papyrus, discovered in the Theban Necropolis, reveals. Invariably, however, the disciplines of botany and magic became entangled, and a brief glance at works such as the *Natural History* of the Roman author Pliny reveals that by Classical times plants were enmeshed in a complex weave of fact and lore.

As society had evolved and hunters settled into being farmers, so the spirit world had become more clearly defined and the mystical role of plants changed. They became symbols of the gods. Classical myth and legend can often reveal the origin of beliefs about many of the plants which still hold special significance today. The Oak became the tree of Zeus and Jupiter, partly through its immense size and strength, but also because of the folklore which surrounded it and which told of lightning strikes, the special weapons of both deities, being attracted to Oaks. The reputation of *Circaea lutetiana*, the Enchanter's Nightshade, owes its beginnings to the story of the goddess Circe, who entrapped the Greek hero, Odysseus, on the island of Aeaea and kept him languishing there through her magical arts and her supernatural use of plant potions. Wormwood and Mugwort, both plants of considerable mystical and protective significance, owe their name *Artemisia* to the guardian Ephesian mother goddess, Artemis. The Paeony is named after the minor god of healing, Paeon, who is named in the Homeric poems as the deity who tended the wounds of the underworld god, Hades. Paeoan is also an epithet for Apollo in his capacity as a healer, and thus the Paeony became a remedial plant which the herbalist, Culpeper, extolled for its value against nightmares and melancholy dreams.

Throughout the Medieval period, for king and commoner alike, there was none of the benefit of modern pharmacy, and people were reliant on less scientific remedies for their ills. Many of these constituted little more than placebos or, at best, the offer of a short-term illusion of cure. In too many cases the so-called 'signature' of the plant was used as a vital benchmark of its medical value. Thus, because the spotted leaves of a particular herb appeared to resemble the tissue of the lung, it became known as Lungwort (*Pulmonaria*) and was used to treat infections of the chest. By similar token, the roots of the Lesser Celandine (*Ranunculus ficaria*), with their approximate resemblance to haemorrhoids, gave the plant the common name of Pilewort and the unjustified reputation as a cure for the painful condition.

Lesser Celandine roots were used to treat piles.

Some herbs, though, did indeed provide sound therapies and are still commonly in use in modern medicine, particularly in homeopathy. Irrespective of the efficacy, or lack of it, in these treatments, they were all that lay between health and suffering, and the herb woman dispensing her 'simples' was an integral and important part of town and village life. Her skills in preparing distillations, infusions, decoctions, ointments and poultices were learned from her mother and grandmother and she, in turn, passed them on to her daughters. She possessed an intimate knowledge of the countryside and of the plants of woodland, hedgerow and field, and would collect her materials at the properly ordained time and in the correct manner. It was recognized that the diary of picking was governed by astrology. Herbs gathered for benevolent purposes were taken beneath a waxing moon, those for maleficent use were collected when it was waning. The best time for obtaining roots, leaves and berries for constructive use was at the full moon and, conversely, when in its darkest crescent herbs were imbued with their most dangerous properties. Thus the witches of Shakespeare's *Macbeth* dug up the root of Hemlock (*Conium*) under the cover of blackest night.

The Old English word for a plant or herb is *wyrt*, but this became changed over the centuries to *wort*, and the corruption has given rise to many of the common names of plants such as Stitchwort, Pilewort and St John's wort. The 'tag' also often offers a clue to their past usage in medicine or magic, since the term for the secret understanding of the properties of herbs was 'Wortcunning'. The traditional image of the cauldron of steaming brew being stirred by a witch generally derives from the pots in which herb women, so often perceived by the Church as witches, boiled their ingredients to produce simples. Throughout the Medieval period, the arts of herbalism, alchemy and magic were difficult to separate, and the herb woman often paralleled her roles of spell-caster and dispenser of home-brewed therapies. The knowledge of the magical use of plants was further broadened as European and Muslim cultures intermingled, and to the old Celtic and Classical lore was added that of the eastern world. This was particularly true in Spain, and through the knowledge gained by the Crusaders in respect of the skills of their enemies.

The magical curative properties of certain plants, and their ability to protect against disease, was not limited to the Medievalists. It was widely accepted until as late as the eighteenth century and, in country districts, often until much later. The old idea of the nosegay, for example, was to carry a sprig of flowers that would keep infection at bay, and one popular children's rhyme was, in reality, a sinister warning about the deadly epidemic against which even a magical posy of flowers might not protect the wearer. Some of the early symptoms of bubonic plague included a ringlike rash and the sneezing by which the bacteria was largely spread:

Ring-a-ring of roses
A pocket full of posies
A-tishoo, a-tishoo, we all fall down.

Very often what appears, at face value, to be little more than a romantic association can contain elements of truth. Contained in the *Folk Lore Record* of 1878 there is an old saying which mothers used to impress upon their children, rather in the vein of a modern 'Green Cross' safety code for crossing the roads. 'Beware of an Oak, it draws the stroke; avoid an Ash, it counts the flash; creep under the Thorn, it can save you from harm.' Statistically the Oak does, indeed, seem to be more prone to lightning strikes than most other trees, and so the logic of assuming that the mighty Oaks were the special trees of Zeus and Jupiter may have grown out of an entirely practical experience. The logic of creeping under a Hawthorn is, however, a purely romantic one, since the Thorn has long been regarded as a holy tree. Sometimes arcane proverbs and sayings can reveal esoteric associations which have otherwise been long forgotten but which, again, possess a germ of accuracy. There is an old country maxim that 'every Elm has its man'. One might imagine this to be an odd turn of phrase but, in fact, it provides a practical warning, the truth of which is revealed in a brief comment in *The Times* of 29 November 1928: 'Owing to the frequency with which this tree sheds its branches, or is uprooted in a storm, it has earned for itself a sinister reputation.' Earlier, the writer Kipling had also noted, less prosaically: 'Ellum she hateth mankind and waiteth till every gust be laid to drop a limb on the head of him that any way trusts her shade.' Less ominous is the quaint lovers' proverb: 'When the furze is in bloom, my love is in tune.' This is a reflection of the observation that Furze or Gorse (*Ulex*) is rarely not to be found in flower!

Plant associations have also given rise to some common metaphors. Perhaps the one which springs most readily to mind is that of 'grasping the Nettle,' meaning the tackling of an unwelcome or unpleasant challenge with firmness and boldness. It originates, of course, in the countryman's knowledge that to grab a Nettle firmly and pull it out will avoid the peril of its stings. Thus we are given the sensible and moralistic advice of W. Secker, writing in *Nonsuch Professor* of 1660, that: 'Sin is like the Nettle, that stings when it is gently touched, but doth hurt not when it is ruggedly handled.'

It was the curative properties of plants, though, which continued to give them their strongest magical and mystical connotations. As late as the time of Thomas Culpeper, the English herbalist writing in the mid-seventeenth century, plants were still considered to be under the dominion of astral bodies and to possess properties which were in accord with these influences. Thus those herbs of a soothing disposition, such as Mallow (*Malva*), were claimed by Venus, while narcotics like Hemlock (*Conium*) were often controlled by the cold presence of Saturn and Mercury, and Jupiter took a hand with species such as Dandelion (*Taraxacum*) that influence the brain or other bodily functions in a positive, opening manner. Mistletoe (*Viscum*), with its golden colour, was predictably under the dominion of the sun. The *Herbals* were compiled in an effort to instruct not only physicians but also ordinary people in the street on how to cure themselves. Some, like Culpeper's *British Herbal and Family Physician – for the Use of Private Families*, were written in the basic language that a poor and semi-literate person could understand.

Long after the demise of the local herbalist's art as a commercial enterprise, most country people would not consider having a garden in which medicinal plants were absent from cultivation, and there are still people living in remote parts of the British Isles who would prefer to collect herbs to remedy their ills before seeking professional medical help. Even in towns and cities, there has been a noticeable drift back towards reliance on herbal remedies over the products of the pharmaceutical industry.

Past beliefs about plants have gone far beyond associations with medicine. A particular tree has often been given a so-called 'life-index' through which its welfare has been seen to be directly linked with that of its owners. If it has become diseased or has been felled, it has been believed that the owner too will suffer misfortune as a reflection of the fate of the tree. By similar token, many plants were believed to possess lucky or unlucky traits and would be either encouraged to grow near houses or shunned. Some were associated with witchcraft and other perceived dangers, while some offered protection to their bearers.

It would be impossible to include all the plants which have, at one time or another, possessed magical or mysterious associations, since to do so would, in effect, be to compile a complete *Flora*. This book examines those species which have been of particular significance and details some of the more common beliefs and traditions associated with them through the ages.

Aconite *(Aconitum anglicum)*

Where and when

Also known as Monkshood or Wolfsbane, Aconite is largely a mountain plant which occurs in damp and shady places at higher altitudes throughout Europe and temperate Asia, extending north as far as the Arctic Circle. In the British Isles the wild form is found in a few localized spots, flowering between May and June. It is, however, very similar to the cultivated exotic varieties of Garden Monkshood (*A. napellus*) that bloom somewhat later.

Appearance

A tall hairless perennial, up to 2 m (6 ft) high and bearing palmate leaves which are cut into five principal pointed segments, each of which is further deeply divided, this being particularly noticeable in the varieties of the garden species. The stems arise from a thick black rootstock and the flowers, which in shape are reminiscent of helmets, are formed in spikes at the tops of the stems, are a dark bluish violet. Monkshood, a member of the Buttercup family (Ranunculaceae) should not be confused with Winter Aconite (*Eranthis hiemalis*), a garden escape.

Traditions and associations

Intensely poisonous, with its toxins concentrated primarily in the roots, and arguably among the most dangerous plants in the British Isles, Aconite has come in for its share of lore and legend, as its other common names suggest. One of the first references to its use appears in Classical Greek literature. On the island of Chios, in the eastern Aegean, one of the alleged birth-places of Homer, men who had reached the age of senility were administered a draught of Aconite as a form of enforced euthanasia. Robert Graves describes a more mythological association of the plant with the entrance to the kingdom of Hades. It was reputed that one of the many gateways to the Underworld was at Heracli in Anatolia and that the Aconite grew where the saliva of Cerberus, the hound of Hell, dripped on the ground. The name Wolfsbane originates in the alleged practice among Anglo-Saxons of dipping arrowheads in the juice prior to wolf-hunting expeditions.

When rubbed into the skin the juice provides a sensation of tingling and then numbness, for which reason Aconite was considered a standard ingredient of witches' 'flying-ointment'. When combined with other narcotic ingredients it may have given the mental sensation of levitation.

Angelica, Wild

(*Angelica sylvestris*)

Where and when

Angelica is common throughout the British Isles, favouring dampish woodlands, but also appearing in a variety of boggy or marshy situations, including roadside ditches. Angelica flowers from July to September. The plant used as the basis of commercial preparations of crystalline sweets is not this species but *A. archangelica*, an introduction to the British Isles from northern Europe, which has become locally established as an escape.

Appearance

A member of the Parsley family (Umbelliferae), Angelica is a perennial herb growing to a height of 1.5 m (5 ft) with erect, branching stems which are ridged and hollow, downy below but otherwise more or less hairless. Among more distinctive features, the stems are suffused by an even purple coloration. Leaves are 2- or 3-pinnate, with the lobes further divided and stalked, the bases of the stalks being expanded to envelop the stem in a sheath. The flowers are arranged in dense, white or pink-tinged umbels, and the individual blooms are very small.

Traditions and associations

Because of its slightly sweet and aromatic properties, Angelica has been used in cookery for many centuries, and the popularity of preserved Angelica is widespread. It also constitutes an essential ingredient in the traditional preparation of Chartreuse and Vermouth. The name Angelica derives from a belief, known from ancient times, that the plant offered protection against bubonic plague. From the fifteenth century, there are records which indicate that it was worn as a charm to combat plague, based on the folk legend that an archangel had revealed its properties to an unnamed visionary, and it was collected regularly from sites around London, including Lincoln's Inn Fields, during the height of the epidemic in England in 1665. According to one author, it blooms by tradition at the Feast of the Apparition of St Michael which, in the old calendar, fell on 8 May. Thus it offers protection against less benign apparitions and witches and, in various parts of Europe, country people have made necklaces of the leaves to give protection to children against demons, enchanters and sorcerers. It has also been regarded as protective against the bite of mad dogs. According to Culpeper, who recommends collection when the sun is in Leo, it has also been described as a herb of the Holy Ghost, although he decries this association as being a Papist blasphemy.

Bay Laurel or Bay Tree

(Laurus nobilis)

Where and when

Although described as a tree, it is more commonly classed as a shrub. The Bay Laurel is indigenous to the Mediterranean regions of Europe and can only be grown in more northerly latitudes if protected from the low winter temperatures. It is altogether distinct from the Common Laurel (*Prunus laurocerasus*) grown in gardens, and is the true Laurel of the Classical tradition. Today, it is grown in pots for its ornamental value and for the culinary use of its leaves, and is more commonly known as the Bay Tree.

Appearance

A small tree growing, in its native regions of southern Europe, to a height of 6 m (20 ft), though in cultivation it is usually pruned into a smaller, more manageable shrub. The branches are clothed with dark glossy green, ovate leaves. The flowers are small and appear in tight clusters in the axils of the leaves.

Traditions and associations

As a handsome evergreen, Bay Laurel was perceived as a symbol of immortality in Ancient Greece and Rome, where it also became the emblem of nobility and victory. It was sacred to several gods, including Apollo and his son, Asclepius, the god of medicine; but Bay Laurel was a plant of Apollo above others. He was linked closely with the natural world, largely because of his habit of philandering with woodland nymphs and virginal conquests of the human kind whom he turned, once deflowered, into flowers and trees of a different sort. As a symbol of victory, Laurel leaves were worn on the brow of every triumphant Roman general as he rode his chariot around the Circus in celebration.

Asclepius, in addition to his symbol of a staff entwined with serpents, also wore a crown of Bay Laurel. He met an unfortunate end when Zeus, in a fit of jealous pique, dispatched him with a thunderbolt, although, in contrary fashion, the tree became regarded as a protection against lightning, since it was reputed never to be struck, and it became a popular insurance decoration in Roman houses. The famous oracle of Delphi, the seer of Apollo, whose name was Pythia, was said to gain her clairvoyance by chewing on the leaves of Bay Laurel and inhaling the smoke of the burning branches, which induced a somewhat frenzied trance.

The withering or diseasing of Bay Laurel was believed to be a portent of disaster. All the laurels in Rome were said to have been blighted, in spite of a mild winter, before Nero torched the city, and from Shakespeare's *Richard III* come the lines: 'It is thought the king is dead; we will not stay, the bay trees in our country are all withered, and meteors fright the fixed stars of heaven.'

In more recent times, the herbalist, Nicholas Culpeper sustained the arguments for the magically protective properties of the tree: 'It resisteth witchcraft very potently, as also all the evils old Saturn can do the body of man, and they are not a few, and I am not mistaken if it were not Mizaldus, that neither witch nor devil, thunder nor lightning, will hurt a man where a bay tree is.'

The Bay Laurel is also symbolic of wisdom and poetry, both attributes of Apollo, an association which is still honoured today in the title Poet Laureate.

Black Horehound

(Helleborus niger)

Where and when

Not a native of the British Isles, but indigenous to southeastern Europe, Black Horehound is nevertheless extensively cultivated and is popular because it is one of the few flowering plants to bloom in midwinter, hence its common English name of Christmas Rose. In the British Isles, the indigenous species include *H. viridis*, the Green Hellebore, and *H. foetidus*, variously known as Stinking Hellebore, Bear's Foot or Setterwort.

Appearance

A low-growing perennial herb with a distinctive rosette of dark green leaves, each with five ovate and somewhat serrated leaflets, which may be covered in a purplish black discoloration which gives rise to the name Black Horehound. The flowers are either solitary or in groups of two or three with five large, showy, petal-like sepals that are white or tinged with lilac, enclosing butter-cup-yellow anthers. It is also claimed that the name Black Hellebore refers to the colour of the roots.

Traditions and associations

Because of the purging action of the juices, all Hellebores have been in medical use since at least 1500 BC, and were often applied to treat children for worms or lice, with fatal results. According to Robert Graves, *Hellebora* means the food of the goddess Helle. In Classical tradition, the plant was said to grow on Mount Helicon, and one of the earliest myths associated with its purging property is that of the Homeric seer and physician, Melampus, the son of Amphythaon and Idomene, who restored the daughters of Proetus, the King of Ephyra, from insanity which had been inflicted by the goddess Hera. He did so by using extract of Black Hellebore accompanied by the sacrifice of a pig, and washing the madness away in a mountain spring flowing at ancient Lusi. In some versions of the mythology, one of the daughters died in the process and Melampus and his brother, Bias, later married one surviving daughter apiece.

For reasons which are not wholly clear,

Hellebores used to be dug up in parts of the British Isles from within a circle drawn in the earth with a pointed object and with invocations to various spirits. They were then used to bless cattle and to rid houses of evil influences. The association with cattle may stem from a practice revealed by Culpeper, who describes the efficacy of boring a hole through the ear of a domestic animal troubled with a cough or which has been poisoned, and inserting a piece of Hellebore root which, he claims, will effect a cure within 24 hours. He suggests that farriers have, in past times, put the plant to other unspecified magical uses.

Less benevolent use has been made of the juice of Hellebore by the Irish Celts, who are said to have dipped their arrow tips in a lethal concoction which also incorporated extracts of Yew and Devil's Bit Scabious. Hellebore-laced arrowheads were also thought to make the flesh of animals slain in the chase more tender.

Bramble or Blackberry

(Rubus fruticosus)

Where and when

Ubiquitous throughout Europe, western and central Asia and parts of north Africa, though not extending to the Arctic Circle or into mountain regions, the Bramble or Blackberry occurs prolifically in woodlands, hedges, scrub and waste places and can form its own isolated thickets. It flowers from May to September.

Appearance

A woody, partially evergreen biennial which spreads by stolons. The stems are branching and tough, at first green, later woody, and armed with hard prickles. The leaves are darkish green, trifoliate and the leaflets are broadly ovate and serrated. The flowers occur in compound cymes; each is made up of five petals which may be white, pastel pink or, sometimes, a deeper shade of pink. The fruit is the distinctive black, shiny collection of fleshy drupelets.

Traditions and associations

The Bramble has been associated with virtue and therefore with numerous quack remedies, and it is one of a number of plants which have been associated, spuriously, with the cure of rupture. A child suffering from the affliction was passed back and forth several times through a natural loop created by the arching-over and rooting of a stolon. This was then bound tightly together in a ritual which was claimed to generate a sympathetic magic. Bramble flowers were also believed to be effective against the most venomous of snake bites, and the briars were used as a charm against whooping cough. Graves notes Bramble in use as a charm against scalding, during which one dips nine bramble leaves in spring water and applies them to the affected area with the accompanying charm: 'There came three angels from the east, one brought fire and two brought frost. Out fire, in frost. In the name of Father, Son and Holy Ghost.' There is, in addition, a taboo against eating Blackberries in certain parts of Brittany and Wales which would seem to derive from ancient Celtic tradition linking the trifoliate Bramble with the triple goddess.

Margaret Baker cites a quaint old notion that it is unlucky to eat Blackberries after Michaelmas Day which, in the old calendar, fell on 11 October. The tradition arose because the Devil allegedly fell into a Bramble bush when he was ousted from Heaven, and spat on the berries on that day in revenge for his physical suffering.

The Devil, it is said, dislikes the Bramble because of its virtuous nature and because, according to some legends, it formed either the Crown of Thorns of the Crucifixion or Moses' 'burning bush'. Having been defeated by St Michael and having nothing more constructive to do with his time, he cursed the plant so that it would never bear fruit until Michaelmas Day had passed. The Devil is also supposed to have trodden an irate path around the Bramble on St Simon's Day, 28 October, so that no berries appear afterwards.

Broom *(Cytisus scoparius)*

Where and when

Not to be confused with the Spanish Broom (*Spartium junceum*), the Common Broom is abundant and widespread in Britain and western Europe, though thinning out eastwards. It favours dry acid soils, including heaths, but is rarely seen on chalk and limestone. The flowers emerge from May to June. Broom is a member of the Pea family or Leguminosae.

Appearance

A shrub growing to a height of 1.5 m (5 ft) with long, more or less straight, erect branches which are conspicuously angled in cross-section. The lower leaves are trifoliate and arise on short stalks, while the upper ones are sessile with the leaflets frequently reduced to one. The flowers are bright yellow, sometimes tinged with red, and showy, arranged in ones and twos along the stem. The fruits are in the form of elongated, hairy-edged pods, which ripen from green to black.

Traditions and associations

Historically, the Broom has strong associations with English royalty. The family name of the Plantagenets derives from the old medieval name of the plant, *Plantagenista*, which was taken up by Henry II. It also appears on the Great Seal of Richard I and was favoured for its remedial qualities by Henry VIII. The delicate buds of Broom, preferably pickled in vinegar, were once considered a delicacy and were on the menu, as appetizers, for the coronation feast of James II. Before the introduction of Hops they were also an essential ingredient of beer-making, used to add the essential bitter tang.

In a number of English counties, Broom has possessed sinister qualities; it was thought an ill omen for the head of the household if the floors were swept with Broom sticks which had blossoms on them. It has never been associated with witchcraft, however; and in other parts of the British Isles the reverse was true, and a bundle of green Broom twigs, tied with a ribbon, was regarded as a symbol of good luck at a wedding.

Celandine, Lesser

(Ranunculus ficaria)

Where and when

This common member of the Buttercup family (Ranunculaceae) occurs in woodlands, hedgerows, fields and waste places generally, throughout Europe and western Asia. It flowers early in the year before many other spring flowers have bloomed.

Appearance

The leaves arise from part-creeping, part-erect, branching stems and are dark green, heart-shaped with slightly lobed margins, and long-stalked. The subterranean tubers are club-shaped. The flowers are pretty, golden yellow and solitary, each with eight or more overlapping petals.

Traditions and associations

The Roman writer Pliny claimed that swallows fed their young with bits of Lesser Celandine in order to improve their eyesight, and among its common names is Swallowwort. A distinct similarity in the shape of the root tubers to that of haemorrhoids, however, has provided the plant with its most curious association, and once gave it the popular name of Pilewort. The principle of sympathetic magic may, in part, have prompted Nicholas Culpeper to remark: 'The virtue of an herb may be known by its signature, as plainly appears in this; for if you dig up the root of it, you shall perceive the perfect image of the disease which they commonly call the piles.' There is, however, a distinct ring of truth here and the herb was, in postwar years, re-introduced into the *British Pharmacopoeia* as a specific in haemorrhoid treatment when made up into a paste. By the same token of sympathetic magic, the yellow juice was once believed to be effective, though less so, against jaundice.

The plant synthesizes juices which are highly irritant to the skin, and there are reports that in bygone times beggars used to rub Celandine into their feet to exact sympathy and cash hand-outs from passers-by.

Chicory *(Cichorium intybus)*

Where and when

Chicory is common across much of Europe and Asia, though mainly restricted to the more temperate regions. It is generally found growing in drier waste places, though in England it appears to grow locally, favouring calcareous soils, typically in rough pasture and along grassy roadside verges. It is rare in Scotland. The flowers appear over several months through late summer and autumn.

Appearance

A tall perennial herb, growing up to 1.2 m (4 ft) in height, the stems either unbranched or with limited, acutely angled branches which are tough, grooved and typically hairy. The leaves are of two types: lance-shaped and stalkless above, their bases clasping the stem; pinnately lobed on short stalks below. All leaves are more or less hairy. The flower is a pretty and distinctive blue which stands out among the predominantly yellow wild flowers of late summer and autumn. Each inflorescence includes a single stalked head at the tip and several stalkless flowers below. A member of the Daisy family (Compositae), the more obvious parts of the flowers consist of blue florets surrounded by bracts.

Traditions and associations

The plant was greatly valued by the Classical Greeks and Romans both for its claimed therapeutic properties and as a vegetable, and it was early Arab physicians who gave it the name 'Chicourey'. The medieval English herbalists knew it as Succory, and for many centuries it was grown in cottage gardens where its remedial properties as an 'opener of humours' were recognized; it was used to assist in recovery from an assortment of afflictions, and to combat such terrors as St Anthony's Fire.

Chicory was also known as an aphrodisiac, the seed being covertly administered to a loved one to make him or her more amorous. There is a quaint, if sad, tale from Germany of a maiden whose lover departed on a long voyage. Day by day thereafter she devoted herself to sitting by the roadside and watching for his return, but he never came back. Eventually she took root and became the 'watcher of the road'. A less romantic slant on the story suggests that her man left her for good reason and gives the plant the alternative name 'accursed maid'.

The best-known use of the root has been as a coffee substitute, but its more magical properties include the power to render a person invisible. Margaret Baker describes an old superstition that Chicory could open locks when a leaf was held against the keyhole, though the plant had to be gathered with considerable ritual and on a specific date, St James's Day, 25 July, or the user would suffer serious misfortune.

Chrysanthemum

(*Chrysanthemum* spp.)

Where and when

The species contained in this large genus range throughout Europe, Asia and parts of north Africa. The old cottage-garden varieties of yellow and white Chrysanthemums derive from a species indigenous to north Africa (*C. coronarium*), while some of the more modern strains have been developed from the Oriental species (*C. sinense*). Ox-eye Daisy (*C. leucanthemum*) is among the more common European species growing in the wild. It is abundant in rough pasture, roadside banks and verges and other waste places, flowering through much of the summer. The plant is also known commonly as the Moon Daisy and the Dog Daisy.

Appearance

Ox-eye Daisy is a perennial herb with more or less unbranched stems reaching a height of 60 cm (2 ft). The leaves are fairly small, dark green and glossy, toothed or serrated. The upper leaves are narrow and partly clasp the stem; the lower ones, held on long stalks, are broader. The flowers, which are large and showy, appear singly, each consisting of a disc of numerous small, yellow florets surrounded by white rays.

Traditions and associations

In Italy, the Chrysanthemum is viewed as a flower associated with death and funeral rites. Various traditions have become associated with Chrysanthemum species in Britain. The Ox-eye Daisy is sacred to St John and it has been considered lucky to step on the first flower of the season. It is also a flower which has come in for other superstitions including the removal of the petals one by one, chanting 'He loves me, he loves me not!'

Clover *(Trifolium spp.)*

Where and when

A genus with a considerable number of members and belonging to the Pea family (Leguminosae). The most common species are, probably, the Red Clover (*Trifolium pratense*) and White Clover (*T. repens*). Both are widespread in waste and grassy places throughout Europe and Asia from the Mediterranean to the Arctic Circle, and are extensively grown as fodder crops, though often as cultivars. Clovers tend to flower throughout the summer period.

Appearance

Mainly low-growing, non-woody perennial plants which bear trifoliate leaves. Red Clover is slightly downy and tends to be erect in habit, while White Clover is wholly hairless and prostrate. The flowers are borne in densely clustered 'pompom' heads, each individual being like a miniature Pea flower with wings and a keel.

Traditions and associations

Clover has long been regarded as a lucky plant because of the religious connotations in its trifoliate leaves, which symbolize the nature of the Trinity. In the past it has been worn as a talisman to deflect the dangers of witchcraft and sorcery. The notion that a four-leaved Clover would bring particular fortunes probably arose from its association with the Cross. These aberrations in leaf form have been relied on for all kinds of magical purposes, including divination and the protection of crops and domestic animals.

Cowslip *(Primula veris)*

Where and when

A member of the Primula family (Primulaceae), the Cowslip or Paigle is found over almost the whole of Europe and western Asia, although thinning out northwards and not penetrating the Arctic Circle. It appears in pastures and other grassy places, mostly on calcareous soils but also on clay, and flowers in spring.

Appearance

A perennial with a basal rosette of leaves and comparatively tall flowering stems. The leaves are primrose-like, though smaller and narrowing sharply towards the base. The flower stalks are leafless and bear delicate, half-pendulous umbels of pretty, yellow flowers, which may be orange-tinged in colour.

Traditions and associations

The Cowslip has long been regarded as an aid to beauty, and Nicholas Culpeper extols this particular virtue lavishly in his *Herbal*. He also suggests that because the Greeks believed the Cowslip to have properties to remedy palsy they named it *paralysis*. In medieval England, this became translated as Palsy Wort, and the plant was kept in high regard for its therapeutic benefits against an assortment of nervous conditions including vertigo, hallucinations, frenzy, epilepsy and other convulsions. In the nineteenth century the cosmetic use was still strong. In a volume entitled *English Wild Flowers* there is the observation that: 'The village damsels use it as a cosmetic, and we know it adds to the beauty of the complexion of the town-immured lassie when she searches for and gathers it herself in the early spring morning.'

The plant also possessed religious connotations, being known as Herb Peter or St Peter's Keys; while in parts of East Anglia more pagan associations were announced by the inclusion of the flowers in the traditional maypole decorations. There was a tenuous rumour that the plant was a lure for nightingales, but the argument proved controversial since it was pointed out that nightingales are 'as common as Blackberries' in parts of East Sussex, where the Cowslip is virtually unknown.

Dandelion *(Taraxacum officinale)*

Where and when

One of the commonest of field and wayside weeds, the Dandelion is ubiquitous throughout the northern hemisphere. It flowers for much of the year but is seen at its best in late spring when it often carpets fields in profusion.

Appearance

A perennial herb growing up to 30 cm (1 ft) in height, with a basal rosette of deeply toothed leaves, and tall leafless flowering stems which bear the solitary, bright yellow, composite flowers. The fruits take the form of the distinctive feathery 'Dandelion clocks'. The green parts arise from a deeply embedded tap root, and all parts yield a milky juice.

Traditions and Associations

The name Dandelion comes from the French *dent de lion,* not because of the shape of the leaves, but because the lion was considered a symbol of the sun and the flower is sunlike. In bygone times, the plant was given the quaint name of 'Piss-a-bed' because of its strongly diuretic properties. The word *Taraxacum* derives from the Greek and means 'to disturb or alter the state of something', which, again, is a reflection on the medicinal effect. One of the first recorded references to the therapeutic use is that of the Arab herbalist Avicenna in the tenth century, and it crops up in the thirteenth century in the *Herbal* of the Welsh physicians of Mydrai. Until the seventeenth century, however, it was valued for its cleansing properties, being a plant under the dominion of Jupiter.

Perhaps the most familiar image of the Dandelion lies in the children's game of telling the time by blowing the fruits off the 'clock'. It has also been regarded as protection against witchcraft when picked on Midsummer's Eve.

Deadly Nightshade

(Atropa bella-donna)

Where and when

Also known as Dwale, the plant originates from southern Europe and west central Asia where it favours waste ground and stony places. It was spread extensively within the areas of Roman occupation, and can now be found extending throughout the milder latitudes of Europe and the British Isles, particularly around Roman archaeological sites and ancient castles and other ruins. It springs from a perennial rootstock and flowers during summer.

Appearance

An erect branching herb which grows into a stout bushy perennial, the stems arching characteristically and bearing large, stalked, ovate, entire leaves. The flowers, borne at the base of the leaves, are solitary, drooping and dull purple with bright yellow stamens. The fruit is a lozenge-shaped berry, about the size of a cherry, which is at first green, then red, and finally glossy black. Deadly Nightshade is a member of the Solanaceae family.

Traditions and associations

The Romans favoured this intensely poisonous plant and dispersed it throughout Europe because of its bizarre cosmetic property. It is from this that the Latin *bella-donna*, meaning 'beautiful lady', originates. As the generic name *Atropa* suggests, the plant synthesizes the alkaloid atropine, which is absorbed very rapidly into the bloodstream and produces a battery of symptoms. A quaint old summary goes: 'hot as a hare, blind as a bat, dry as a bone, red as a beet and mad as a hen', all of which is moderately accurate. Among the effects, which can readily be fatal if enough of the berries are consumed, is the dilation of the eye pupils. The ladies of the Roman aristocracy came to appreciate this, and a distillation of the Deadly Nightshade juices was prepared which could be dropped into the eyes to make them appear large, dark and appealing. It is a well-recorded medical phenomenon that enlarged pupils are an outward sign of sexual hormonal stimulation and that the condition produces a positive response in the opposite sex. In reality, the effect would have presented more of a glassy, staring appearance with the pupils more or less immobile, unless the dosage was measured very carefully.

In later times, in Buckinghamshire, the Deadly Nightshade fruits became popularly known as 'naughty man's cherries', according to Curtis' *Flora Londinensis*.

The poison is known to be ingested with full immunity by a range of herbivorous animals, but it also appears that it can be passed on in this way. It is alleged that it can be accumulated in the honey of bees which have foraged extensively on Deadly Nightshade pollen, and there are unsubstantiated reports of people suffering symptoms of atropine poisoning after consuming the contaminated meat of rabbits which have presumably been grazing on the plant leaves. The common name 'nightshade' derives from the dangerous narcotic effects of the plant: it first stimulates the nervous system and then paralyzes it.

In controlled amounts, extract of Deadly Nightshade possesses a therapeutic value, and has been recognized in the treatment of poisoning by another alkaloid, muscarine, one of several occurring in the Fly Agaric mushroom (*Amanita muscaria*). Tincture of Belladonna has, until very recent times, been a staple of the pharmacist's stock-in-trade.

Dog's Mercury

(Mercurialis perennis)

Where and when

A commonly occurring weed of woodlands and hedgerows throughout Europe and western Asia, which flowers in early spring.

Appearance

The simple unbranched herbaceous stems arise from a slender creeping rootstock, grow to a height of about 20 cm (8 in), and are clothed with slender, ovate leaves, which are finely hairy and serrated. The flowers develop in the axils of the leaves, starting before the latter have fully opened. The green, petalless flowers are borne on separate male and female plants, the male inflorescence taking the form of a distinctive spike, the female being less conspicuous and arising in groups of two or three.

Traditions and associations

Like a number of sexually distinct wild plants, Dog's Mercury has attracted connotations of fertility. The Greek physicians Dioscorides and Theophrastus developed the fanciful notion that the sex of an unborn child could be determined and controlled through the use of this plant. If a woman takes either the male or the female plant in a decoction over a three-day course of treatment after conception, it is claimed that she will give birth, respectively, to either a boy or a girl. Hippocrates did not subscribe to this particular piece of nonsense, but did recommend Dog's Mercury for a host of 'women's problems'. It was probably called Dog's Mercury to distinguish it from the slightly larger Annual or French Mercury. Though supposed to be a plant of the Greek god Mercury, Nicholas Culpeper claims its properties to be more in keeping with a herb of Venus.

Fennel *(Foeniculum vulgare)*

Where and when

Fennel is probably of southern European origin, but because of its popularity as a cultivated herb it has spread northwards over many centuries and is now found in the wild across much of temperate Europe and Asia. Although it grows mainly in dry stony places close to the sea, Fennel frequently strays inland, though probably more as a garden escape. In its typical habitat, it is found most commonly on grassy cliffs and swards, creating large feathery clumps. In the British Isles, it tends to peter out towards the north and is not found naturalized in Scotland or Ireland. Fennel flowers in the late summer and early autumn.

Appearance

A tall perennial with erect, branching, slightly ridged stems up to 1.5 m (5 ft) tall, bearing finely dissected leaves with very narrow, almost capillary leaflets. The leaf bases sheath the stems, which are hollow when old. Towards the end of summer, the large, loosely arranged umbels of small, yellow flowers emerge. The whole plant possesses a distinctive aroma of aniseed.

Traditions and associations

An old English proverb declares 'Sow Fennel, sow sorrow' but, on the whole, the plant has been viewed as a boon rather than a curse. The herbalists were full of praise for its remedial properties in treating anything from snake bites and mushroom poisoning to gout and obesity. It was equally of value in dispersing kidney stones and curing flatulence. A further therapeutic use lay in healing eye infections, and there exists a delightful old English herbal rhyme, preserved in Stockholm, which extols the benefits of Fennel to serpents with failing eyesight!

Whaune the neddere [adder] is hurt in eye
Ye rede fenel in hys prey,
And zif he mowe it fynde,
Wonderly he doth hys kynde.
He schall it chow wonderly,
And leyn it to hys eye kindlely,
Ye jows schall sawg and hely ye eye
Yat before was sicke et feye.

In Longfellow's *Goblet of Life*, Fennel takes on a more martial role in addition to restoring eyesight:

Above the lowly plant it towers,/
the fennel with its yellow flowers
And in an earlier age than ours/
was gifted with wondrous powers
Lost vision to restore.
It gave new strength and fearless mood,/
and gladiators, fierce and rude,
Mingled it in their daily food,/
and he who battled and subdued,
The wreath of fennel wore.

The extensive spread of Fennel may, in part, be explained by the edict of the Emperor Charlemagne, crowned Emperor of the West in AD 800, that the plant was to be cultivated on all the imperial farms. Fennel sprays were also incorporated into the crown of victory for Roman generals parading in the Circus.

The plant has been held as a protection against witchcraft and malevolent spirits and, to this end, it was hung over doorways on Midsummer's Eve. In the lore of the horsemen, a sprig of Fennel tucked into a harness was claimed to keep flies at bay.

Ferns

Where and when

Generally speaking, the various species of fern grow in cool, shady conditions in woodlands, hedgerows and on or near walls, where there is a plentiful supply of ground water.

Appearance

Most ferns take the form of a rootstock or rhizome, from which roots descend and leafy fronds are produced. The fronds not only synthesize food but also bear the reproductive organs on their margins or surfaces.

Traditions and associations

Almost all the magical and mysterious associations lie less with fern plants than with their tiny, almost invisible 'seeds', which are more properly defined as spores. The seed of ferns was once considered not only rare but possessing mythical and marvellous strengths which were at their most powerful during the summer and winter solstices, during which it generated homeopathic properties allied to gold and fire. At Christmas it was seen to symbolize the hidden fire of the winter sun, while in summer it could only be collected within three days of Midsummer's Eve when it was reputed to glow like gold or yellow fire. This golden attribute has led to many bizarre stories about the treasure-seeking powers of fern seed. James Frazer cites a Bohemian saying that 'on St John's Day fern seed blooms with golden blossoms that gleam like fire' and describes the myth that whoever holds it on Midsummer's Eve and climbs a mountain will discover a vein of gold or see the treasures of the earth bathed in blue flames. In Russia there has been a similar tradition that, if fern seed is tossed in the air on Midsummer's Eve, treasure will be found buried at the spot where it falls.

In some of the old Medieval textbooks, fern seed was also believed to have the property of rendering invisible a person who swallowed it, as well as conferring other magical abilities such as defence against evil spirits, thunder and lightning. This belief encouraged the growing of ferns on the walls and roofs of houses. It was also believed to have antidote properties against snake bites.

Foxglove *(Digitalis purpurea)*

Where and when

The Foxglove is common over large parts of western and central Europe, where it is found in woods, waste places and hillsides, favouring acid soils. It is not commonly found in limestone regions. Foxgloves are also frequently cultivated in gardens for their showy spikes of flowers. The flowering period extends from June to September.

Appearance

An unbranched perennial or biennial bearing soft and broadly lance-shaped leaves on the tall stems, at the top of which tapering spikes of flowers appear. In the wild form, these are pinkish-purple, typically spotted inside the corolla tube and shaped like the finger of a glove. In garden cultivars, the colours of the flowers are more varied.

Traditions and associations

The assortment of common names for Foxglove provide some indication of the range of its magical and mysterious links, since it has also been known as Dead Man's Bells, Bloody Fingers, Fairy Caps, Fairy Gloves, Fairy Thimbles, Virgins' Gloves (this particularly from France) and Witches' Gloves.

Records of the interest in the Foxglove go back to at least Anglo-Saxon times, and it is found in an official list of curative plants dating from the reign of Edward III. The cures with which it was credited were largely spurious, and often positively dangerous, because the plant synthesizes digitalin and other related and toxic chemicals known as glycosides which have a cumulative effect on the human body. The main effect is on the action of the heart, causing it, when administered in excess, to fibrillate and eventually to fail. It was, however, brought to the attention of the medical fraternity again in the eighteenth century by the Warwickshire physician, William Withering, and was widely used in pharmacy until after World War I, particularly as a remedy for the condition known as dropsy. When Withering died, a Foxglove was carved on his tombstone in the graveyard of an Edgbaston church. In earlier times, it was also believed to clear up ailments ranging from itches and phlegm to leprosy. In less beneficial applications the juice was used as an ordeal poison and to treat the tips of hunting arrows. The flowers are incorporated in the emblem of the Clan Farquharson.

In England, popular legend has it that the sinister attributes of the Foxglove were first discovered by a witch in Shropshire, although a more appealing story tells that the wicked fairies are supposed to have given the flowers to the equally wicked foxes so that they could tiptoe around the chicken runs without giving themselves away.

Dead Man's Bells is a Scottish name which derives from the odd notion that a person close to death could hear the 'bells' of the Foxglove ringing, and it has always been considered unlucky to bring a Foxglove into the house north of the border.

Heather (*Erica* spp.)

Where and when

A perennial evergreen undershrub which, in its various native species, is widespread on heaths and moors, though some are more localized than others. Most flower during summer, but some of the imported varieties which are found in gardens are winter-flowering. All these undershrubs are members of the Heath family or Ericaceae, which includes Ling.

Appearance

The *Erica cinerea* or Bell Heather (illustrated) generally grows up to 40–50 cm (16–20 in) tall, although other species including Irish Heath (*E. mediterranea*) can be much bigger. The leaves of Bell Heather are small, dark green and linear, with their margins rolled under as a device to protect against water loss. They are generally borne in whorls of three. The flowers are oval 'bells' and are arranged in longish spikes. In the wild form they are typically purple.

Traditions and associations

The name Heath or Heather derives from a Christian missionary association, since the plant commemorates the efforts made to convert the heathen Picts to Christianity. The evangelists preferred to use force of arms before reason and effectively coerced the opposition. The Picts willingly went to the defence of their beliefs and gave battle; thus the hillsides were drenched with the blood of the heathen which, so goes the story, became Heath.

The notion of White Heather as a lucky plant was popularized by Queen Victoria. There is a record that in 1862, while staying at Balmoral, she presented Princess Alexandra of Denmark, the wife of the future Prince of Wales, with Heather, saying that it would bring her good fortune. The story goes that the White Heather escaped being stained by the blood of the ancient battlegrounds. There is a thriving cottage industry cultivating the white varieties for popular

demand, although gypsies still prefer to sell Ling.

At the turn of the nineteenth century, Heather tops were still used in a thriving brewing industry to ferment a local Scottish beer. It was traditionally made in August and September and also incorporated hops, ginger and syrup. Heath used to be cropped to stuff mattresses in such places as Dorset, too.

Hemlock *(Conium maculatum)*

Where and when

A biennial herb which grows in tall, elegant clumps and can be found in a variety of damp locations in meadows, hedgerows and verges and in open woodlands. It is reasonably common throughout the British Isles, Europe and temperate Asia. It flowers in late summer.

Appearance

Erect and branching, the plants can grow to a height of 1.5 m (5 ft) or more, and are clothed with large leaves, strongly divided into ovate segments. The upper leaves tend to be smaller with less obvious divisions. The stems are hollow and spotted distinctively purplish. All parts emit an unpleasant smell when bruised. These two characteristics tend to separate the true Hemlock from a number of other Umbellifers which are loosely referred to by the same name.

Traditions and associations

Small quantities of Hemlock can be fatally poisonous to humans and many other creatures. Hemlock came to achieve notoriety in Classical Greece when it was employed as the official instrument of execution for political prisoners found guilty of serious crimes against the state. Its most famous victim was, undoubtedly, the philosopher Socrates. He had been an advocate of the radical and disruptive belief that true knowledge is only acquired through dialogue, which effectively ran against the principles of tyranny. In 339 BC he was accused of impiety and corruption of youth and condemned to take a lethal draught of Hemlock.

According to contemporary reports, Socrates was fully conscious until the end, and the mysterious associations gained by the plant have been enhanced by the nature of the poisoning which, in effect, is not unlike that of the South American arrow toxin, curare. It causes paralysis of the nervous system, allegedly affecting the extremities of the body first, rendering them numb, and gradually extending inwards until death ensues from heart failure and respiratory collapse through the breakdown of regulatory centres in the brain.

Administered in a less disastrous cocktail, Hemlock is also said to have been employed in the Mysteries performed in Eleusis. These rites included a Sacred Marriage during which intercourse took place between the High Priest and Priestess of the goddess, Demeter. Theirs, however, was a symbolic act during which the libido of the Priest was kept within the bounds of propriety by the numbing effect of the drug.

Hemlock was an ingredient of the witches' brew in Shakespeare's *Macbeth*. As with many magical plants used for evil purposes, it had to be collected at night, and is thus described as 'root of hemlock digged i' the dark'. Banquo subsequently complains: 'Have we eaten of the insane root that takes the reason prisoner?'

Since it possesses a strong narcotic effect, Hemlock was also one of the herbs from which juices were extracted to prepare the so-called 'flying-ointment' of Medieval witches. In his book *De Miraculis Rerum Naturalium*, the sixteenth-century Neapolitan writer, Giovanni Battista Porta, who wrote in Latin, includes the name *eleoselinum*. Some authors have interpreted this as Hemlock, although a more likely translation may be Parsley (within which family Hemlock is a significant species).

In medicine, the extract of the plant has long been recognized as a sedative and, in more recent times, as an antidote to strychnine poisoning. Culpeper, in his *English Physician and Complete Herbal,* offered a more bizarre therapeutic use for the plant with echoes of its Classical value. He suggested that a cold poultice of the leaves 'applied to the priveties' acted as a kind of early bromide, curing lustful thoughts.

Henbane *(Hyoscyamus niger)*

Where and when

Henbane occurs throughout the milder regions of Europe and western Asia. In Britain, it is not a particularly common plant in modern times, though it is more prevalent in locations in southern England where it grows on sandy soil near the sea, typically favouring ground which has been recently disturbed. Henbane used to grow extensively around old-fashioned middens and where slops or 'common jacks' had been thrown out, and has been known by a variety of common names, including Jupiter's Bean and Devil's Eye.

Appearance

A herbaceous biennial growing 50–80 cm (20–32 in) tall, with an erect, unbranched stem clothed in soft, white hairs. The leaves are alternate and of two types, the upper ones being narrowly ovate, toothed and stalkless, and the lower ones more broadly ovate, less obviously toothed and stalked. Both types are hairy. The flowers, arranged in terminal rows, possess yellow or cream corolla tubes patterned with lurid purple veins, and have leafy bracts at their bases. The fruit is a smooth, green capsule encased in a five-toothed cup.

Traditions and associations

The Greek physician Dioscorides was probably among the first to identify the medicinal value of Henbane, and the Roman historian, Josephus, implies that the headdress of the Jewish high priests was modelled on the fruit of the plant, which gives an indication of the mystical respect in which it was held as a pain-killer. The Romans would appear to have introduced Henbane into Britain, respecting its analgesic properties, particularly during childbirth.

In England, during earlier centuries, an improbable form of quack dentistry was associated with the plant. This involved an elaborate piece of trickery which appeared to produce an effective, if short-duration, magical cure for toothache. Seeds of Henbane were heated in water in a chafing dish, over which the patient suffering from toothache was positioned. The toothache would be miraculously cured and in the bottom of the dish appeared 'worms' which were claimed to have fallen out of the rotten teeth! Gerard's *Herball* includes the cynical observation:

> *...drawers of teeth who run about the country and pretend they cause worms to come forth from the teeth by burning the seed in a chafing dish of coals, the party holding his mouth over the fumes therof, do have some crafty companions who convey small lute strings into the water, persuading the patient that these little creepers come out of his mouth.*

Henbane contains an active component in the form of the alkaloid hyoscyamine, which has a similar effect on the human nervous system to scopolamine. While all parts of the plant are poisonous, the greatest concentration of this chemical occurs in the seeds. In sober reality, the heat applied to the seeds caused them to split open and the tiny white plumules to spring out, while the narcotic fumes of hyoscyamine temporarily anaesthetized the nagging tooth. The pain did not return again until the quack dentist had claimed his fee and sent the patient on his or her way.

Iris (*Iris* spp.)

Where and when

A number of species of wild Iris grow in the British Isles, including the familiar Purple and Yellow Water Flags, *Iris versicolor* and *I. pseudacorus*, the Stinking Gladwin or Roast Beef Plant, *I. foetidissima*, and the related Spring or Autumn Crocuses, *Crocus purpureus* and *C. nudiflorus*. Cultivated varieties, however, outstrip the native forms, and most of these derive from European species, most particularly those with showy flowers such as *I. susiana*, *I. sibirica* and *I. germanica*.

Other than the spring and autumn species, Irises generally flower between June and August.

Appearance

The typical cultivated Iris possesses long, narrow leaves that arise from a creeping rhizome. The flowers are borne on long, leafless stalks and show a complex arrangement of petals including falls and standards.

Traditions and associations

The Iris is named after the Greek messenger goddess. A virgin deity, she attended the goddess Hera and was responsible for the rainbow bridge between heaven and earth. She also carried the souls of women to their place in the other world. For this reason the Classical Greeks planted Iris around their tombs. In later times, in Spain, the white varieties of Iris became a symbol of the Immaculate Conception, and, from an innovation of Charles V, in poetry its typical three flowers were interpreted as faith, wisdom and courage.

The Iris is one of the most widely known emblems of heraldry, since it is the model for the Fleur de Lys. The story goes that Louis VII of France dreamed of Irises before setting out on the Crusades in 1137, considered this to be an omen, and therefore adopted the flower as his emblem. It became known in France as the Fleur de Louis, having had the earlier title of Fleur de Luce. Finally it became the Fleur de Lys through corruption. The emblem was also popularized in England by Edward III, although it was dropped from the national standard at the onset of the Napoleonic Wars early in the nineteenth century.

In early medicine, Iris was considered good for everything from snake bites to coughs and bruises, and at the turn of the twentieth century the English firm of Leghorn and Paris had a thriving business exporting up to 20 million 'beads' or portions of Iris root each year as a cure for scrofula and blood diseases.

Ivy *(Hedera helix)*

Where and when

A strong and prolific climber which will readily utilize tree trunks, rocks, walls and other manmade brick or stonework as a support, Ivy has the distinction of coming into flower just as most other vegetation is dying away for the winter months. It is common throughout western and southern Europe and extends through Asia as far as Japan, though it is more rarely seen in central Europe.

Appearance

A woody evergreen whose branches may spread along the ground or climb on suitable supports, using small root-like protuberances called *haustoria* with which to attach itself. These do not absorb water or minerals and merely act as a means of support. The leaves are glossy, dark green and variable in shape, palmate, except on the flowering shoots, where they are ovate. They appear in alternate arrangement and are stalked. The flowers, which emerge between September and December, are small and green with tiny, yellow stamens, and are arranged in umbels. The berries which form in late winter and early spring are at first green, ripening to dull black.

Traditions and associations

In the Classical literature, Ivy is a plant of both Dionysos and Bacchus, respectively the Greek and Roman gods of wine, and in *Attica* a famous Dionysos Ivy is mentioned growing at Acharnae. In one mythological tale, Dionysos punished a crew of pirates for their impiety towards him by turning the oars of their ship into serpents and filling the vessel with Ivy, causing them to lose their sanity and drown themselves. James Frazer refers to the Bacchanals who gained intoxication through eating Ivy. The priest of the god Jupiter, among many taboos, was forbidden to touch or even to utter the name of the plant. Robert Graves, in *White Goddess*, describes how, in the Bacchanalian orgies which took place in Thessaly and Thrace during the month of October, the Bassarides wrought intoxicated havoc, tearing animals and human children alike to pieces in their drunken frenzy while carrying Fir boughs entwined with Ivy. This perhaps also explains the claim that Orpheus was torn to pieces by a pack of ferocious women drunk on Ivy. The plant was sacred to other deities including the Phrygian god, Attis, whose emasculated priests, the *galli*, were tattooed with Ivy-leaf patterns, and to the Egyptian god of the dead, Osiris.

Ivy has also provided the basis of an intoxicating drink which was popular during the Medieval period and was, until recently, still brewed at Trinity College, Oxford, in memory of one of their past students who was killed by hooligans from Balliol.

Predictably, the early Christian Church took a dour view of the various uses of Ivy, fallacious and otherwise, because of the pagan connotations, and in some counties it was always banned from forming part of the Christmas decoration in churches. It has been claimed to possess properties of fertility, not an ideal attribute in Christian terms, and it is one of many plants that was popularly regarded as a safeguard against witches when grown against the wall of a house. It seems somewhat illogical that Ivy has also, in past centuries, gained a spurious reputation for preventing drunkenness. In the taverns of the Middle Ages, however, wine goblets were traditionally carved from Ivy wood, although Ivy-wood cups were also considered efficacious against whooping cough, perhaps because the wood contains a narcotic alkaloid, hederine.

The traditional Christmastide battle between the Holly and the Ivy has been given more than one interpretation. One possibility lies in the old English tradition of binding the last sheaf of the harvest with Ivy and describing it as the Harvest Bride or the Maid of the Ivy, which was said to bring ill luck in the following season to the farmer who had been late with his harvesting. By contrast, the first-footer over the doorstep on Yuletide morning was a dark youth known as the Holly boy, who was said to bring good fortune. Thus the Ivy Maid and the Holly Boy became traditionally opposed.

For many centuries the leaves of the plant have also been regarded as an efficacious narcotic and as a useful treatment for wounds. People often chewed Ivy leaves as a cure for toothache, and Leonardo da Vinci describes a widely held belief among country people in Italy that wild boars were reckoned to go away and roll in beds of ivy when wounded in the hunt. A decoction of Ivy berries in a vinegar was also considered to be a specific remedy against the plague. For sufferers from corns, either a few leaves popped into the shoes overnight or binding the affected parts with leaves soaked in vinegar would, it was claimed in different parts of the country, make the corns vanish overnight!

Lady's Smock *(Cardamine pratensis)*

Where and when

This delicately attractive plant of late spring and early summer often carpets damp water meadows or the edges of roadside ditches, as well as woodland margins. It is very common throughout Europe, northern Asia and Canada, and can be found at altitudes up to 1,000 m (3,000 ft).

Appearance

A perennial herb with clusters of pale lilac flowers at the top of unbranched stems, up to 50 cm (20 in) tall. At the base of the stem is a rosette of pinnate, long-stalked leaves with rounded leaflets; the leaves on the upper part of the stem are short-stalked and narrowly lance-shaped, arranged in a spiral. The flowers each bear four petals and are stalked, and the fruits are in the form of conspicuous siliquas with little beaks which disperse their contents by explosion.

Traditions and Association

An alternative common name for Lady's Smock is Cuckoo Flower, as it is one of a number of spring flowers that appear more or less with the arrival of the cuckoo in Britain. It has also been called Cuckoo Spit Flower because, although in reality the familiar white froth is produced by a plant bug, it was believed that cuckoos flying overhead spat on the plant and therefore made it unlucky, particularly for husbands of errant wives. Shakespeare tells, in *Love's Labour's Lost*:

When daisies pied and violets blue,/
and Lady's Smocks all silver white
And cuckoo buds of yellow hue/
do paint the meadows with delight
The cuckoo then in every tree mocks married men,/
for thus sings he, Cuckoo!

There have been strict taboos about when Lady's Smock can and cannot be used for decoration. Its incorporation into Mayday garlands was traditionally strictly forbidden, as was bringing the flowers into the house. If it was discovered in a garland, the entire decoration had to be destroyed. There is some argument that this avoidance was on account of an association with fairies of evil disposition.

The quaint name Lady's Smock may come from the appearance of large masses of the flowers in a meadow when viewed from a distance. Washing was often conveniently dried by spreading it out on grass, and the flowers may have looked like a week's airing laundry! In some country districts it has been tagged 'bread and milk', from a custom of breakfasting on bread and milk in the spring when the flowers appear.

In medicine, Culpeper describes the plant as being under the dominion of the moon, good for scurvy and an excellent tonic for bucking up a lost appetite. Other therapeutic uses have included combating epilepsy.

Lords and Ladies

(Arum maculatum)

Where and when

Known by various alternative names (see below), the plant is found in woods, thickets and hedgerows throughout much of Europe and the British Isles, thinning out substantially in more northerly regions. It flowers in the spring and its distinctive red berries are conspicuous when other vegetation dies away in the autumn.

Appearance

Arising directly from a tuberous white rootstock, the leaves are more or less arrow-shaped with lobes at the base, and are borne on long stalks reaching an overall height of as much as 50 cm (20 in). The leaves are dark green and may be characteristically spotted purple. The flower takes the form of a paler green spathe, 15–25 cm (6–10 in) long, which tapers at the top and which conceals the spadix or spike. This is club-shaped and yellow or purplish and, when ripe, becomes a cluster of bright red berries in a short spike on a naked stalk or peduncle.

Traditions and associations

The diversity of common names attached to this striking plant, including Adder's Root, Arum Lily, Cuckoo Pint, Friar's Cowl, Kings and Queens, Starchwort and Wake Robin, point to a wealth of lore and legend. One of the earliest associations comes from the Greek writer, Aristotle, who suggested that bears emerging from hibernation used the plant to soothe sore paws which had been chewed on through the winter months to ease hunger pangs! Because of the appearance of spotting on the leaves, this plant was, by tradition, one of those which grew at the foot of the Cross and on which dropped the blood of Christ.

Although poisonous in the raw state, the root tuber is both edible and highly nutritious when cooked, and in past times it was collected and eaten. It became almost a staple fare among the local people on the Isle of Portland. The herbalist Gerard describes the starch made from the roots as, 'The most pure and white . . . but most hurtful for the hands of the laundresses that have the handling of it, for it chappeth, blistereth and maketh the hands rough and rugged and withall smarting'. The making of the starch went out of fashion but was rediscovered towards the end of the eighteenth century by Jane Gibbs of Portland in Dorset. During the nineteenth century a flour was manufactured from the roots, and marketed as Portland Sago or Portland Arrow Root. In Switzerland, juice extracted from the fresh roots has been used as a soap substitute, and the gay Parisiennes of earlier days applied the dried and pulverized roots to their faces as a cosmetic aid called Cyprus Powder. In various countries the juice was believed to remove freckles. More prosaically, a mixture of the berries and hot ox dung was considered remedial when slapped onto gouty limbs. Arum decoctions were also believed good against the plague, probably because of the religious connotation, although in Cambridge bringing the plants indoors was thought to afflict anyone who went near them with tuberculosis.

The imagery of phallus and sheath has offered many sexual connotations and thus has given rise to such local names as Kings and Queens, Lords and Ladies and even Dog's Dick. In parts of Dorset it was believed that girls who touched the plant would become pregnant. Elsewhere, young men would place a piece of the plant in their shoe as a certain means of obtaining a girl's attention! It has also been known as Parson in the Pulpit, and in Devon it has been called Snakes' Meat, deriving from the legend that adders obtain their poison from the plant by eating the berries.

Mandrake, English

(Bryonia dioica)

Where and when

A common hedgerow climber belonging to the Cucurbitaceae or Cucumber family, it is better known as the Common or White Bryony. It occurs throughout the central and southern areas of Europe and the British Isles, though it is not present in more northern latitudes, including Scotland. It is also absent from Ireland, and is rare in Wales. Flowers appear during summer and the fruits are distinctive features of the autumn hedgerow. White Bryony is, incidentally, quite distinct from Black Bryony (*Tamus communis*), which has dark, shining, entire leaves.

Appearance

White Bryony possesses weak annual hairy stems, arising from a perennial rootstock, that ramble and branch through stronger vegetation and are clothed with leaves that are deeply divided into five to seven broad lobes. The flowers are small, male and female separate. The males are clustered on stalks and pale yellow; the females are smaller and generally borne in pairs. The berries are red, their surfaces matt, and contain several flattish seeds.

Traditions and associations

Popularly known as the English Mandrake or Devil's Turnip, White Bryony is an altogether separate species from the true Mandrake (*Mandragora*) which belongs to the Solanaceae family and which is sometimes grown as an ornamental exotic.

One of the earliest references to the magical value of English Mandrake comes from the Classical era when Augustus Caesar occasionally wore a circlet of Bryony around his head as a protection during thunderstorms. There is also some tenuous suggestion that the juice was administered by Roman soldiers as a 'Death Wine' to crucified victims; in this context, it may have been one of the earliest forms of anaesthetic. It is, however, the anthropomorphic shape of the root and the remarkable dimensions to which it can grow that has prompted much of the bizarre lore about this plant. In his *Herball*, Gerard describes, 'A root hereof that weied half an hundredweight, and of the bignes of a child of a yeare old.'

In days gone by, a cunning deception involved exposing the rootstock of a young plant and shaping around it a clay mould in the shape of a human trunk and legs. The earth was replaced and the root left to develop, conforming to the restricting outline. At the end of the season it was dug up, accompanied by a level of ritual, and at precisely the right time of day and in proper weather conditions. The shape, when revealed, was like that of the true Mandrake in distinctly human form. Local superstition claimed that the root, which was reputed to grow only during the hours of darkness, shrieked like a soul in agony when ripped from the ground. One of the more fanciful tales suggests that the shriek was so awful to the human ear that a dog was tied to the root and encouraged to pull it up. The roots were judged to be male or female, according to individual shapes and attributes.

The Mandrake has long been regarded as being among the most magical of plants. In the Far East it is revered for its supposed aphrodisiac properties, and it has been resorted to in European sorcery and witchcraft as a plant that will enhance psychic abilities and divinatory powers.

The therapeutic use of the plant has long since ceased, since all parts synthesize dangerous toxins including the alkaloid bryonine. In past centuries, however, an extract of the berries was employed to treat open sores or 'tetters', hence another old common name of Tetterberry, and there are records of Greeks and Romans using it to alleviate painful conditions such as gout, jaundice and rheumatism.

Marsh Marigold

(*Caltha palustris*)

Where and when

A member of the Buttercup family (Ranunculaceae), Marsh Marigold flowers throughout the spring and early summer, from March until June. Although its range stretches throughout the temperate regions of Europe and Asia, it is more or less confined to wettish places in both fields and woods, particularly favouring boggy stream banks, where it often forms extensive showy clumps.

Appearance

A perennial herb growing to 40 cm (16 in) in height, Marsh Marigold has partly creeping and partly erect stems arising from a thick, creeping rhizome. The leaves are large, roughly triangular and glossy with bluntly toothed margins, more or less sessile above but on long stalks below. The flowers are large, showy and shining golden yellow, either solitary or borne in clusters of two or three.

Traditions and associations

The assortment of common names including King Cups, Horse Blobs, Water Blobs and Verrucaria offer some measure of the popularity of this attractive spring plant. Like others that bloom at the same time of year, it has featured in Mayday celebrations, and was a source of protection against witchcraft on Mayday Eve or Beltane. One of its local names in the Isle of Man was *Lud y Voaldyn* or *blughtan*, which means 'the herb of Beltane'. It has, conversely, been an unlucky plant to bring into the house prior to the first of May. It also had its benevolent uses, though. In Ireland it was often used, in company with Rowan blossoms, to garland a hoop from which two balls were suspended. According to Frazer these were covered in gold and silver paper and perhaps, with the gold and white blossoms, represented the sun and moon. Bunches were hung in houses during May as a protection against lightning and, if picked with a certain ritual and carried about on the person, it has been believed that the bearer will be protected from having angry words spoken of him or her.

The common name of Verrucaria stems from a past therapeutic use when the burning juice of the plant was applied to warts.

Meadowsweet

(Filipendula ulmaria)

Where and when

Also known as Queen of the Meadows, this common perennial occurs in meadows, field borders, roadside verges and on the banks of ponds and streams throughout the British Isles, Europe and western Asia, except in the far north. It flowers throughout much of the summer.

Appearance

A member of the Rose family (Rosaceae), Meadowsweet grows up to 1.2 m (4 ft), in height, with stiff, upright hairless stems clothed with large, pinnate leaves, each carrying five to nine narrowly ovate segments. The stems of this perennial are topped by delicate and attractive masses of small, yellowish-white flowers, which are sweetly and strongly fragrant.

Traditions and associations

As with many white or creamy flowers, particularly those that are strongly perfumed and have small petals which fall creating an obvious litter, Meadowsweet bears an association with death. Until very recent times, in parts of England, the scent of the flowers was believed under certain circumstances to induce a deep and fatal sleep. It has also been seen as a fatal flower in Wales, and Robert Graves notes that the plant is one of nine, along with Oak, Broom and others mentioned in the Welsh saga of *Llew Llaw Gyffes*, from which Blodeuwedd, Llew's wife, was created. In Irish tradition the moon goddess Aine of Knockaine, in whose care lay the wellbeing of crops and cattle, gave the Meadowsweet its beautiful smell.

The blossoms used to be dried and smoked like tobacco in Nottinghamshire, where they were called Old Man's Pepper. 'Old Man' is a common tag for the Devil.

Mistletoe *(Viscum album)*

Where and when

Seen in its best-known state at Christmas, when it bears its white berries, this parasitic and somewhat woody evergreen plant has three distinct races, of which only one is common throughout temperate Europe, and which grows mainly on the branches of apple and poplar, often very high up. It is much less frequently seen on its traditional host, the Oak. In the British Isles, it is not found in Scotland or Ireland. It is now cultivated extensively as a Christmas decoration. Other races which are very rare in Britain grow on coniferous trees.

Appearance

Dense, much-branched tufts reach 30–60 cm (1–2 ft) across, and sprout from the bark of the host plant by way of a thickened base. The branches are at first succulent and yellowish-green, but become woody in older specimens, and the leaves are more or less ovate, thick and leathery-fleshy. The flowers are very small, with tiny petals. The male and female inflorescences are separate and both emerge in the forks of the branches. The berries are white and semi-transparent and consist of a soft, somewhat sticky flesh surrounding a single seed.

Traditions and associations

Culpeper sums up one of the paradoxes of this curious and highly magical plant when he comments:

> *It can be taken for granted that that which grows upon oaks participates something of the nature of Jupiter, because an oak is one of his trees . . . but why that should have most virtues that grows upon oaks I know not, unless because it is rarest and hardest to come by.*

Whether Mistletoe on Oak was more common in the Celtic era from which its associations largely spring is unclear, but the Roman writer Clusius states that, in his day, it was at least as common on Pear trees. It is also Clusius who provides the essential instruction that the Mistletoe that has been cut should not be allowed to touch the ground. Culpeper observes that, when worn around the neck, it provides a specific protection against witchcraft.

Mistletoe has long been regarded as an efficacious medicinal plant. The Druids valued its healing powers and the Roman historian Pliny wrote that the Celts called the Mistletoe 'all-healing'. He noted at least 11 conditions which could be treated by the plant extract, including the dispersal of tumours. It is interesting that traces of Mistletoe have been analyzed from at least one Bronze-Age tree coffin burial in Yorkshire and from the bog corpse unearthed at Lindow in Cheshire. Lindow Man, dating back to about 300 BC, had consumed Mistletoe immediately before his ritual execution, and the fact that he had Mistletoe remnants in his stomach has always been taken to indicate some kind of ritual meal. He may, in fact, though, have been an early cancer-sufferer treating his condition.

It is unclear how far back in European prehistory the veneration of Mistletoe can be traced, but Pliny also mentioned its use in the treatment of epilepsy, which used to be known as the 'falling sickness' and which, because of its symptoms, was regarded as a demonstration of possession by evil spirits. In 1720, Sir John Colbatch wrote a pamphlet detailing its use with epileptics. It has also been considered effective as a mild heart stimulant and useful in the lowering of blood pressure, although modern medical opinion agrees that it is more or less worthless.

In mythology, although Frazer maintains that Mistletoe is one and the same as the Golden Bough, which Virgil describes Aeneas plucking at the behest of the Sibyl before setting out on his voyage to the land of the dead, it is the natural

historian Pliny who probably sheds the most comprehensive light on the value of Mistletoe in the Classical period.

In a mystical context, we can be sure that the Celts held the Oak in much the same sacred regard as did the Romans, and thus their Druidic priesthood came to hold the Mistletoe in great veneration. Again, however, it is Pliny who offers the only real contemporary insight into the attitude of the Druids towards the plant. He writes of the Druids that they believe whatever grows on the Oak trees is sent from heaven and is a sign that the tree has been chosen by their god himself.

> *The mistletoe is very rarely to be met with; but when it is found they gather it with solemn ceremony. This they do above all on the sixth day of the moon, from whence they date the beginnings of their months, of their years and of their thirty years' cycle because by the sixth day the moon has plenty of vigour and has not run half its course. After due preparations have been made for a sacrifice and a feast under the tree, they hail it as a universal healer and bring to the spot two white bulls whose horns have never been bound before. A priest clad in white robes climbs the tree and with a golden sickle cuts the mistletoe which is caught in a white cloth. They then sacrifice the victims, praying that God may make his own gift to prosper with whom he has bestowed it. They believe that a potion prepared from the mistletoe will make barren animals to bring forth, and that the plant is a remedy against all poisons.*

It is on this one observation that much of the more recent mythology about Mistletoe is based. Pliny also makes it clear that Mistletoe should not be cut with a knife made of iron, and should not be allowed directly to come in contact with the ground. Perhaps predictably, he also confirms that the Mistletoe which grows on Oak possesses the strongest curative powers. The exact purpose of the Druid ritual is unclear, though Robert Graves asserts that it is symbolic of the emasculation and deposing of the old priest of the sacred grove by his more youthful successor. This would explain the slaughter of the white bulls, the symbolism of which is vague, although it is thought that they were seen as potent symbols of masculinity.

The other main source of Mistletoe mythology rests with the Norse sagas and, in particular, in the tragic tale of the god Balder. Balder, 'the shining one', was the favourite son of the father of the gods, Othin, and his end is described in two essentially conflicting ways by rival historians, Snorri Sturluson and Saxo Grammaticus. Whatever deeper logic lies behind its veneer of tragedy, it is unquestionably the slaying of Balder which presages the end of everything, the Ragnarok or Day of Doom.

According to Snorri, Balder experienced premonitory dreams of his own death, which he confided to his mother, Frigg. She, in response, took oaths from all things that they would not harm Balder and, subsequently, it became an entertainment to throw things at this impervious golden youth. Disguised as an old woman, Loki, the half-god, half-giant, whose loyalties lay in more than one camp, probed Frigg to find out if anything had escaped her insurance plan, and learned that the Mistletoe, apparently too frail to cause any harm, had not taken the oath of fealty. On the fateful day, Loki handed a sprig of Mistletoe to the blind god, Hod, and instructed him to use it in the playful target practice. As Hod hurled the projectile it became a lethal dart and Balder fell dead.

Saxo Grammaticus, by contrast, depicts Balder as a lustful demi-god tyrant and warrior, 'sprung from celestial seed' and guarded by Valkyries, who is, nonetheless, slain by a rival possessing a magic sword. This is the version of events which Richard Wagner apparently adopted in *Der Ring des Nibelungen*, transposing Balder for the tragic hero Siegfried, and creating an assassin in the guise of Hagen.

The veneration of Mistletoe has not waned. Frazer described how, in parts of Europe, Mistletoe might not be cut from the tree but was to be knocked loose with stones, or shot free with bow and arrow. Traditions were particularly prevalent in Switzerland and in parts of Scandinavia where the old beliefs in its efficacy as a wound-healer and a universal panacea against poisoning persisted until recent times. It has persistently been viewed as a fertility symbol and in various parts of Europe there has been a tradition of feeding a sprig to the first calf born in the year, to ensure the health and fecundity of the whole herd.

Perhaps the strongest mystical association from Medieval times onwards lies in the effectiveness of Mistletoe as a protection against sorcery and witchcraft. It was also considered to be an effective protection, through its links with the Oak and therefore Zeus and Othin (deities associated with electrical storms), against thunder and lightning, and was hung in houses. It is still regarded very much as a lucky plant, which may explain why the focus in the Christian calendar has shifted from midsummer, the time when it was collected by the Druids, and it has now become an integral part of the Christmas and New Year festivities, when people wish themselves luck for the coming year. To kiss one's sweetheart under the Mistletoe is to bring luck on the future of the relationship and is essentially a relic of the old fertility connotations. Because of its pagan colours, it has long been banned from the Christmas decorations of churches, the curious exception being the Minster of York where on Christmas Eve a large bunch was carried to the high altar and deposited there until Twelfth Night. Among witches and other pagans, however, its modern mystical association still lies with fertility, the festivities of the summer solstice and the figure of Jack-in-the-Green who is decorated, in part, with sprigs of Mistletoe.

Some of the Druid mythology associated with Mistletoe may have more than a vestige of truth associated with it. Recently scientists in Britain and in Russia have established that the plant generates a chemical similar to ricin, which is used in chemotherapy against certain types of cancer. Research is now in progress to develop an effective form for therapeutic application.

Mugwort *(Artemisia vulgaris)*

Where and when

A weed, related to the Wormwoods and the garden Tarragon, which is common in waste places and on roadside verges throughout the northern hemisphere. It flowers in the latter part of summer and through the autumn.

Appearance

A robust, faintly aromatic perennial growing up to 1.2 m (4 ft) in height, with ribbed, somewhat woody, branched stems which may be flushed purplish, and clothed with deeply pinnate leaves, stalked at the base and sessile above, their undersurfaces characteristically downy-silver. The flowers are greenish, small and compactly ovate, arranged in branched spikes.

Traditions and associations

Mugwort has always been associated with midsummer. In company with Mullein, it was believed to offer protection against witchcraft and sorcery in the sixteenth and seventeenth centuries, but was also an important ingredient in the magic of witches and wizards. According to some reports, the juice of the plant was applied to the witch's magical mirror or other scrying device to aid clairvoyance, and it was burnt as an incense under similar circumstances. According to Thomas Hill's *Natural and Artificial Conclusions*, a rare coal is to be discovered under Mugwort, but only during one hour in the day and one day in the year. To find it and place it under the pillow will bring dreams of a future husband. In the Fen district of East Anglia it was known as Lad's Love and, if a young man cut a sprig of it and placed it in his buttonhole before promenading around the village of an evening, it showed that he had romance in mind.

In parts of Europe it was known as the herb of John the Baptist, and in Cockayne's *Saxon Leechdoms* it is said of Mugwort:

Thou hast might for three and against thirty.
For venom availest for plying vile things.

The plant has been associated variously with Venus and with Diana, the goddess of the moon, a link emphasized by the silvery texture of the undersurfaces of the leaves. Venus is sometimes depicted with a spray of Mugwort in her hand. Some of the old herbals also named the plant *Mater Herbarum* (the mother of herbs) and a decoction with Rosemary and Camphor was an old hair tonic.

Mugwort was believed to aid the passage of travellers. The Roman writer Pliny said of it: 'The wayfaring man that hath the herb tied about him feeleth no weariness at all and he can never be hurt by any poisonous medicine, by any wild beast, neither yet by the sun itself.' This belief persisted. According to the 1656 essay, *The Art of Simpling*, by William Coles, a sprig of Mugwort placed in the shoes before setting out on a journey is an aid to offsetting fatigue. The wearer will travel 40 miles before noon without tiring.

Nettle (*Urtica* spp.)

Where and when

One of the commonest weeds, the Nettle is generally distributed throughout the world, and related plants include Hemp, Fig and Mulberry. The Small Nettle (*Urtica urens*) and Common Nettle (*U. dioica*) are familiar throughout the British Isles and Europe, while the Roman Nettle (*U. pilulifera*) is largely confined to the Mediterranean region. Often favouring nitrogen-rich soils, Nettles grow more or less anywhere the ground is left untended, flowering chiefly in summer and autumn.

Appearance

The Common Nettle grows from a perennial creeping rootstock with erect stems up to 90 cm (3 ft) in height, bearing serrated leaves that are ovate below and lance-shaped above. The whole plant is clothed in stinging hairs. The greenish, wind-pollinated flowers, which are separate male and female but generally on the same plant, are borne in spikes that arise from the axils of the leaves.

Traditions and associations

The word Nettle is perhaps a corruption of the Saxon *noedl*, meaning a needle. Because of the burning nature of the juice which is injected through the stinging hairs, Nettle seeds were carried by the Roman legions, whose troops were presumably unaware that the northern climes produced their own species of the plant. They nevertheless believed that flagellation with switches of Nettles was a necessary tonic to the circulation and the general health of the body and, specifically, an aid to the relief of rheumatism, in the unhealthy outposts of the Roman Empire. For the herbalist Gerard, Nettles stewed with sugar made 'the vital spirits more fresh and lively', while for Nicholas Culpeper the seed offered a remedy for the stinging of venomous creatures, the biting of mad dogs, the poisonous qualities of Hemlock, Henbane, Nightshade, Mandrake or similar herbs that dull the senses.

Nettle juice has long been regarded as a tonic and there is an old rhyme which advises:

Sup Nettles in March and Mugwort in May
And many fair ladies won't go to the clay.

Opium Poppy

(*Papaver somniferum*)

Where and when

A native of the Mediterranean region, the Opium Poppy has been extensively cultivated and occurs as an escape generally in Europe and the British Isles, growing in waste places, particularly in fens and adjacent to the sea. It flowers throughout the summer.

Appearance

A handsome erect annual growing to a height of 1.2 m (4 ft), the Opium Poppy bears coarsely toothed leaves which clasp the unbranched stems. All the green parts are more or less hairless and have a somewhat waxy appearance. The flowers are large with lilac petals, each with a more purplish spot at the base, though in cultivars the colour can be richer and more varied. The fruit capsules are rounded and distinctively large containing, when ripe, black seeds which are released from pores beneath the 'crown'.

Traditions and associations

The true Opium Poppy is a distinct species characterized by more or less white petals and a large non-splitting capsule. It is hardly ever seen in the British Isles, but originates in central and eastern Europe and Asia. The British plant is correctly *Papaver somniferum* subsp. *hortense*, which bears a close similarity but does not synthesize the narcotic principles to the same extent in the immature capsule.

In mythology, the Opium Poppy is the plant of sleep and dreams, the word 'morphine' deriving from the Greek word for *form* from which also derived Morpheus, one of the thousand children of the god Hypnos, and a minor deity who took human form and showed himself to people during their dreams. According to Greek myth, the gods caused the Opium Poppy to spring up around the goddess Demeter as she searched vainly for her abducted daughter, Persephone. As she knelt to examine these curiously beautiful growths more closely, she inhaled their bitter aroma and was tempted to taste their seeds. Thus the gods bestowed rest on the anguished Corn Mother (see page 72).

The earliest medical reference to the use of the Opium Poppy may come from Theophrastus, writing in the third century BC, who described it as 'meconium'.

The subsequent spread of the Opium Poppy through the Middle East to Turkey, and on to India and China, was largely accomplished by Arab traders. Though first used as a sedative, its properties as a narcotic drug rapidly brought it to notoriety, and its illicit use must have claimed countless thousands of lives through the centuries. The Arab physician Avicenna was one of the more celebrated individuals who, by repute, died from an overdose of opium, in AD 1030. It was also offered to the dead since it symbolized sleep.

In the nineteenth century, the Opium Poppy was the object of the so-called 'Opium Wars', which were conducted by Great Britain, and later by France, against China, to force the opening of ports such as Shanghai in order to trade in opiates. Opiates originated mainly in British India and were being used to pay for British imports from China, including tea and silks. Until the early years of this century a tincture of opium dissolved in alcohol, known as 'laudanum', was extensively employed by physicians as a sedative. More recently, the great social scourge of modern civilization, heroin, has been synthesized from crude opium.

The word 'Poppy' probably comes from the Saxon *popig*, which stems from the same root as *pap* and suggests that child-bearing women may have mixed Poppy seeds with breast milk to send their infants off to sleep!

In more modern literature there are hints that Sherlock Holmes was addicted to opium, and many members of Victorian society were dependent on it. In quack remedies, because of its narcotic properties, opium has been used to 'cure' a variety of afflictions including toothache, earache and headache. Culpeper recommends it as a treatment for St Anthony's Fire (ergotism).

Parsley *(Petroselinum crispum)*

Where and when

One of several members of the Parsley and Caraway family (Umbelliferae), the cultivated Parsley is a native of the eastern Mediterranean region which has escaped from gardens and become naturalized in many places, often close to the sea among rocks. It flowers in summer.

Appearance

A hairless, bright green biennial which becomes characteristically yellowish with maturity. The stems are full and grow to a maximum height of about 50 cm (20 in). They bear three-lobed leaves, which in the cultivated varieties are very crisped and crinkly. The small flowers are borne in umbels and are greenish-yellow.

Traditions and associations

Parsley is extremely slow to germinate, and probably for this reason a curious tradition has grown up around it. There is a very old country saying that the seed of Parsley goes to the Devil nine times before it germinates. Thus in 1658, in *Wit Restored*, the observation appears that in the North Riding of Yorkshire Parsley is a plant with hellish associations: 'The Weed before it's borne nine times the devill sees.' Apparently it used be thought to visit the Underworld a mere seven times, but the number of trips was increased because of the sacred connotations of the number seven.

In various parts of Britain the plant has been associated with curious taboos. It could safely be sown or planted only on Good Friday, when the Devil was unable to exert his influence over it, but, while it was considered safe enough to be grown in one's own vegetable plot, it would bring disaster if transplanted to anyone else's garden. Also picking it while uttering an oath against another person would have them dead within the week. Conversely, Parsley seed was considered by Culpeper and other herbalists to be particularly effective as an antidote against 'the venom of any poisonous creature', while the boiled roots were efficacious for curing flatulence and as a diuretic, and the juice was an early remedy for sore eyes.

Periwinkle *(Vinca major)*

Where and when

Of the Greater and Lesser Periwinkle, the former is probably more common as a garden escape which has become naturalized in hedgerows, woodland edges and other shady places throughout Europe as far as the Caucasus. It is more common in central and southern Europe and flowers in late spring and early summer. The Lesser Periwinkle is more localized.

Appearance

Long-trailing and rather weak stems are clothed with entire ovate leaves. Unlike the Lesser Periwinkle the stems are not rooting. The flowers are comparatively large and showy, bluish-mauve, each with five petals and a bell-shaped corolla tube.

Traditions and associations

In several countries of Europe, including Britain, France and Italy, the Periwinkle has been a flower closely associated with death. This association came about not on account of its colour, but because of the binding tendency of the stems. In Medieval times those condemned to execution were sometimes given a wreath of Periwinkle before ascending the scaffold. This tradition may date back to Celtic times since, in the story of the ill-fated Llew Law Gyffes of Welsh mythology, the Periwinkle formed an integral feature of his sacrificial rites.

As one of the flowers of death, its tincture was also recommended as a homeopathic remedy against snake bite. Because of its morbid association it was believed unlucky to remove the plant from a graveyard – to do so would be to incur the wrath of the ghosts which haunted the place.

In total contrast the Medieval writer Albertus Magnus included Periwinkle as an ingredient of an aphrodisiac recipe!

Primrose *(Primula vulgaris)*

Where and when

This pretty yellow herald of spring is prolific in woodlands and hedgerows throughout the British Isles, ranging into mountainous regions and onto coastal cliffs. It also extends through much of central Europe, although not generally the northeast, and it can be found in mountainous regions of southern Europe. It flowers throughout the spring months but may also be seen in bloom, occasionally, during mild winters.

Appearance

A basal rosette of thickish, crinkly, lance-shaped leaves develops from a perennial rootstock. The flowers are borne on long, slender stalks and are pale yellow, sometimes tinged pink, with darker nectar guides. To avoid self-pollination, the flowers are of two types – pin-eyed and thrum-eyed – according to whether the stigma is more prominent than the stamens or vice versa.

Traditions and associations

As a flower of the spring, Primrose has collected around it a not-unfamiliar set of taboos and rituals. The Elizabethan poet John Donne wrote a celebrated ode in honour of the Primrose as a flower sacred to the ancient Muses and the quintessence of womanhood. It was claimed to be first grown around the Muses' retreat on the slopes of Mount Helicon. It has also been associated with protection against witchcraft, and it was therefore believed advisable to pick the flowers on the eve of Beltane, the 1st of May, and to display them in a vase in the window.

For some reason it was believed unlucky to pick fewer than 13 in a bunch, and one of my first personal recollections, as a small child picking Primroses with my mother in a wood near our village of Findon in Sussex, shortly after World War II, was to watch her count the flowers in my fingers. She would not allow me to return home carrying less than 14 or it would bring bad luck during the year.

The Primrose (not to be confused with the Evening Primrose) has also had a medical value. In past times the leaves were pounded and made into a salve which possessed excellent curative properties for wounds.

In 1883, the Primrose League was founded in England in memory of and to support the ideals of Benjamin Disraeli, the Victorian prime minister who lived from 1804 to 1881. The Primrose was his favourite flower, and the League instigated a tradition of wearing the blooms on 19 April, the anniversary of his death.

The *Oxford English Dictionary* describes the 'Primrose path' as being the path of pleasure, although Shakespeare makes the trenchant observation that such a route is illusory: 'The puffed and reckless libertine himself the primrose path of dalliance treads.'

Roses *(Rosa spp.)*

Where and when

Wild roses, which include a considerable number of true species, are found growing throughout the northern hemisphere, although they are better known for their garden forms, some of which are of considerable antiquity. Five species are probably indigenous to the British Isles – Field Rose, Dog Rose, Downy Rose, Scotch or Burnet Rose and Sweet Briar – but most garden roses have been developed as hybrids from wild plants of exotic origin.

Appearance

The Field Rose (*Rosa arvensis*) is typical in that it is a clambering, deciduous shrub with pinnate leaves and bears hooked prickles on the long, trailing stems. The flowers are showy and shallowly cup-shaped, while the fruits take the form of bright red 'hips'. Other species vary in the arrangement of prickles, flower colour, hip character and other small features.

Traditions and associations

The Rose, because of its bitter-sweet paradox of sharp thorns and delicate blooms, has earned romantic associations. To the Greeks, the red Rose was dyed by the blood of the goddess Aphrodite when, as she hastened to tend the wounded Adonis who had been fatally gored in his annual encounter with a wild boar, she trod on a white damask Rose bush and ripped the flesh of her foot. In other Classical mythology it is recorded that, as Cupid danced among the gods, he spilled some of his nectar 'which, on the white Rose being shed, made it forever after red'. Among the traditions of Muslims, the red colour of Roses has likewise been seen to be symbolic of the blood of Mohammed, and by the token of its association with blood the red Rose has become a flower associated with martyrs. It should be mentioned that the Rose of Sharon described in the Biblical *Song of Solomon* is not a Rose but a species of the *Hypericum* or St John's Wort genus.

The Rose is also a plant of valour. In the German fairy tale of *Sleeping Beauty*, the hero who awakens the princess after her 100-year magical sleep is obliged to battle his way through a Thorn forest which has fatally impeded others.

As he penetrates deeper so the Hawthorns become transformed into Roses.

Following the Wars of the Roses in which the red and the white Rose were adopted as emblems by the Houses of Lancaster and York respectively, the red Rose became the emblem of England, and was traditionally worn on 23 April, St George's Day.

The old nursery rhyme of 'Ring-a-ring of Roses' (see p.12) has little to do with the Rose, though it does rely on the powers of certain flowers to protect against disease. The title refers, in reality, to the ring-like inflamed rash that appeared prior to the onset of the more severe symptoms of the deadly bubonic plague. The 'pocket full of posies' was believed to offer protection to the bearer, and 'a-tishoo, a-tishoo' proclaimed the sneezing by which the germ was spread before 'we all fall down.'

Rosemary *(Rosmarinus officinalis)*

Where and when

Native to the Mediterranean regions, Rosemary is not hardy enough to withstand severe northern European winters. It flowers in spring and is often found growing near the sea. The name *Rosmarinus* bears no connection with the Virgin Mary, as might be imagined, but simply means 'sea dew' in Latin.

Appearance

A smallish bushy shrub growing to a height of no more than 1.5 m (5 ft), with woody, four-sided, angular stems and a profusion of long, narrow, greyish green leaves which produce an aromatic oil. The flowers are blue, two-lipped, the lower lip having three lobes, and they emerge in whorled, branching spikes from the axils of the leaves.

Traditions and associations

A plant of considerable therapeutic value to the herbalists of bygone times because of the remedial properties of its aromatic oil. By repute it was a holy plant which flowered at the old date of Christmas, 6 January (before the reform of the Julian calendar to fall in with the Continental Gregorian system), although it bears no close associations with the Virgin Mary and its religious connotations are largely of non-Christian origin. The Romans used it to crown their guests at banquets and it was incorporated into funeral rites as well as wreathing household gods. Roman farmers applied the smoke of Rosemary to purify their flocks of sheep. Its fragrance was also believed to preserve cadavers and the lasting green of the leaves made it a natural symbol of immortality, thus there was a fashion to plant it around tombs. Vestiges of this funerary association have persisted from Roman times in parts of northern England where Rosemary is carried in funeral processions and sprays are thrown onto the coffin before the grave is filled.

Rosemary is also a more general plant of remembrance, finding its way into bridal sprays, and it has been popular as a Christmas decoration. The only known association with the Virgin Mary is a tenuous apocryphal story that Rosemary bushes hid her and the infant Jesus from the soldiers of Herod. This protective role in legend has, however, been credited to several plants, including Juniper, and Rosemary is generally a plant of pagan interest. Thus, for example, in Sicily, there exist old traditions that

tell of fairies concealing themselves beneath Rosemary bushes.

Nicholas Culpeper, born in 1616, viewed it as a sovereign remedy and noted that the flowers and leaves made into a conserve provided a specific against bubonic plague. So popular was the herb that in the worst years of pestilence, 1603 and 1625, the price of a bunch of Rosemary in the London markets became inflated to a price beyond the reach of most people. Today, in a distant reflection of its attributed powers to combat infection, the Queen's posy includes Rosemary when she dispenses to the poor on Maundy Thursday.

The plant was also considered to provide luck in love and could be divinatory in determining a young girl's future. If she and two of her intended bridesmaids, all of whom had to be less than 21 years of age, got together on the Eve of St Magdalen to dip sprigs of Rosemary into a cocktail of vinegar, wine, gin and rum, fasten the sprigs to each other's brows, take three sips (no more) and go to bed without speaking, the resulting dreams would tell all!

Rosemary was also a good protector against many of the familiar tribulations and dangers of more mundane life, including lightning and malevolent spirits.

Thorn Apple *(Datura stramonium)*

Where and when

One of a small genus of shrubby plants which extend over the warmer regions of the globe. Around the Mediterranean, it is to be found as a common roadside weed, but further north, as in southern England, it becomes very intermittent in frequency and is generally regarded as a casual of waste ground. It is also plentiful in North America, where it goes under the name of 'Jimson Weed'. Thorn Apple flowers from July until the first frosts of autumn.

Appearance

A scruffy annual with an unpleasant smell and distinctive spiny fruits, it grows up to 1 m (3 ft) in height and is hairless. The leaves are more or less ovate but jaggedly toothed or pointed-lobed, arising from spreading and forked branches. The flowers are white (less frequently purple) and tubular or trumpet-shaped, and the fruits are large, green, chestnut-like capsules which are prickly or spiny and contain wrinkled seeds. It is a member of the Nightshade family (Solanaceae).

Traditions and associations

The Solanaceae synthesize alkaloids which have a pronounced effect on the human nervous system when ingested and some bizarre tales surround the Thorn Apple. The historian Lewison states:

> *We find these plants associated with incomprehensible acts on the part of fanatics, raging with the flames of frenzy and fury, and persecuting not only witches and sorcerers but also mankind as a whole. Garbed in the cowl, the judge's robe and the physician's gown, superstitious folly instituted diabolical proceedings in a trial of the Devil and hurled its victims into the flames or drowned them in blood.*

In other words, for meddling with Thorn Apple you could find yourself burned at the stake.

In some societies it has been used as a so-called ordeal drug, although its use was accompanied by a certain amount of underhandedness. A favoured combatant might be given a cup of wine which had been carefully mixed with the Thorn Apple poison lying in the stem. Having drunk a little, he would deliberately swirl the liquid and hand the cup to his opponent. It has also been employed as a non-lethal Mickey Finn added to beer or wine to produce an effect similar to severe intoxication, and so to facilitate robbery of a victim. In South Africa, where it is known as *laughboontjie*, schoolchildren have used it to mischievous effect as part of an initiation ritual.

The toxins are particularly concentrated in the seeds and they include hyoscyamine, hyoscine and atropine. The combination when consumed causes mental confusion and can, in the later stages of poisoning, cause maniacal behaviour for protracted periods. Consumption of a large quantity of the seeds is needed, however, for death to occur.

In North America, Jimson Weed has been used by generations of medicine men as a narcotic and pain-reliever, but it has also been respected in a more esoteric function. When the spirits were called upon to bring rain, a man would chew on a piece of the root obtained from his shaman while he prayed for rain. There is also at least one legend among the Indians to explain the origin of the Jimson Weed. The plant is said to be a descendant of a boy and girl who strayed into the sacred council grounds of the spirits and then related to their parents what they had seen and heard. Angered, the spirits changed the children into the plants and so, by eating Jimson Weed, others continue to reveal the secrets of the spirits.

In the Far East, Thorn Apple, dried and smoked like tobacco, has been utilized for thousands of years to alleviate the symptoms of asthma, while, in a more sinister application, hyoscine was reputedly the poison used in the notorious Crippen murders.

Thyme, Wild *(Thymus drucei)*

Where and when

Wild thyme is common on dry, hilly grassland, although it thins out somewhat in the southeast area of England, except on chalk downland. It is widespread throughout Europe and north and central Asia, and is generally considered to be subdivided into three distinct types: Common, Large and Breckland Thyme. These species are distinct from the Garden Thyme, *Thymus vulgaris*, which comes from southern Europe and does not overwinter in more northerly climates. Wild Thyme flowers in late summer, mainly from June to August.

Appearance

A prostrate, strongly aromatic, herb which forms mats or cushions specially adapted to minimize water loss and thrives in dry habitats. It spreads by means of underground runners. The stems are short, moderately hairy, and square in profile, bearing small, short-stalked, tough, oval leaves in opposite arrangement. The small, lipped, deep reddish purple flowers are massed in domed terminal heads.

Traditions and Associations

In terms of more practical uses, the Large Thyme is welcomed in sheep pastures, since sheep will browse on the foliage and the aromatic taste is said to be imparted to their meat.

Thyme bears a curious association with death, probably because the flowers are sweet-smelling, and it has been associated with funeral rites, particularly in Wales where it is very common. The flowers are brought into the house in mourning and are kept there until after the burial has taken place. The Order of Oddfellows follows a tradition whereby at the interment of a deceased member his colleagues carry sprigs of Thyme to cast into the grave, and Thyme is believed to favour the places where victims of violent death have fallen. It is certainly true that gypsies have regarded it as an unlucky plant to bring indoors. In the safety of the open air, however, it has been used as an old quack treatment for whooping cough, boiled in water with a little vinegar added and then drunk cold.

It was a popular therapeutic herb in other remedies, a decoction made with vinegar being considered to cure headaches when rubbed into the scalp, and it has also been widely recommended in the herbal treatment of depression.

Vervain *(Verbena officinalis)*

Where and when

Vervain extends throughout much of Europe and Asia, while in the British Isles it is found mainly in the southern counties, and is absent from Scotland. It grows on waste ground and roadside verges and flowers in summer and autumn.

Appearance

An upright, more or less hairless perennial, growing up to 60 cm (2 ft) in height, with somewhat untidy and wiry branches. The leaves are stalked and deeply cut on the lower part of the stem, but are sparse, sessile and lance-shaped above. The lilac or blue flowers are very small, arranged in long slender spikes, and not unlike those of the Mints, members of the Labiatae family, in structure.

Traditions and Associations

Long associated with magic, Vervain was believed by the ancient Persians to possess aphrodisiac properties, and it has been an ingredient of many potions and quack remedies. In English tradition, however, according to J. White in *The Way of the True Church* (1610), the plant had to be gathered to the accompaniment of the correct charm:

Hallowed be thou Vervain,/
as thou growest on the ground
For in the mount of Calvary there thou was first found
Thou healest our Saviour, Jesus Christ,/
and staunchedst his bleeding wound,
In the name of the Father, the Son, and the Holy Ghost,
I take thee from the ground.

As in the case of so many medieval charms, this is clearly a corruption of some early English prayer, the origins of which have been lost.

The extent to which it was valued as a love philtre and charm is indicated by the fact that, in Germany, a wreath of Vervain was traditionally presented to the newly married bride.

James Frazer relates a cure for cancerous tumours based on principles of homeopathy and signature and employed by Marcellus of Bordeaux, the court physician to Theodosius I. It requires cutting a root of Vervain in half, hanging one end around the patient's neck and suspending the other in the smoke of a fire. It is alleged that, as the root shrivels, so will the tumour. A caveat is added, however, that if the patient proves a poor payer, the dried root can be thrown into water, whereupon it, and the tumour, will swell and be restored. In England, Vervain worn around the neck was believed to possess similar properties, according to the *London Pharmacopoeia* (1837), which prescribed it as a remedy for the King's Evil. It was a widespread safeguard against infection in general to hang a piece of Vervain around the neck of a child, though it is unclear whether, in this context, it was regarded more as a magical talisman or as a medicinal herb.

In Germany in the early sixteenth century, on the occasion of St John's Eve at midsummer, people wore garlands of Vervain and Mugwort which they tossed into a bonfire with the words 'May all my ill luck depart and be burnt with these'.

Vervain was considered unusually protective against evil influences and, in England, Vervain garlands and posies were worn to guard against witchcraft, blasting and other misfortunes. It was also hung above thresholds in company with equally popular plants such as Dill and Rowan. Vervain was considered to impede the work of witches and sorcerers yet, paradoxically, it has also been associated with witchcraft as a magical herb of salves and ointments.

There has also existed a curious belief that pigeons and doves pluck Vervain and eat it to improve their eyesight; it has thus been known, in parts of England, as 'pigeon grass'.

Wheat *(Triticum sativum)*

Where and when

Wheat is included here as representative of several cereal grasses including Oats (*Avena*) and Barley (*Hordeum*). All derive from wild grasses which have been grown as crops since prehistoric times and were probably first experimented with in the ancient Near East. All are members of the Graminae family and description of their appearance is probably unnecessary, though it is worth observing that the flowerheads of Barley are upright and tight while those of Oats are loosely branched, spreading and nodding, both with long bristles. The flowerheads of Wheat are not unlike those of Barley, but have comparatively short bristles.

Traditions and associations

Most of these have arisen in association with significant moments in the calendar of sowing, germination and harvesting. In ancient Egypt,

the god Osiris, though best known as the god of the dead and the Underworld, began his career as a vegetation deity who developed Wheat and Barley from their wild state into cultivated varieties, and thus gave humankind the staple fare of Corn to steer them away from hunting and casual foraging. The honour of this discovery is attributed by the Classical writer, Diodorus Siculus, to the goddess Isis, at whose festivals sheaves of grain were carried in procession. James Frazer recounts that when the Egyptian reapers cut the first of the crop they laid down their sickles and beat their breasts crying to Isis and lamenting the execution of the Corn Spirit. This association explains why, in Classical tradition, the goddess Demeter (Greek) or Ceres (Roman) became the Corn Mother, and both she and her ill-fated daughter, Persephone, are depicted in art with garlands of Corn on their heads and holding Corn stalks in their hands. A magnificent image of Demeter once stood commandingly over the threshing floor at ancient Eleusis, the site of the Mysteries.

The theme of the Corn Mother became almost universal throughout pagan Europe and the traditions have remained firmly entrenched amongst country people across the centuries of Christian belief. In many areas the growing Corn is perceived as the temporal embodiment of the Corn Mother or the Corn Spirit, and when it waves in the spring breezes the goddess is believed to be passing by. At such times children are warned against picking flowers in the cornfields or the Corn Mother will catch them.

There was a traditional blessing of the Wheat by young men and girls after they had taken Communion on Palm Sunday. Plough Monday represented a fertility ritual to ensure the fertility of the cereal crop, and the Rogation rituals in April were a familiar scene in many parishes, vestiges of old pagan rites to secure good weather and crop fertility. Villagers walked around the bounds armed with crosses, banners and bells to drive off malevolent spirits and bless the crop. In some places passages from the Gospels were read in cornfields for the same purpose.

At harvest the last few stalks of the Wheat possessed great spiritual significance, because the spirit of the Wheat was believed to reside in them, although the traditions that arose varied according to whether the spirituality was perceived as the repulsive Hag or Crone aspect of the dying year or the infant germ of the new season. Often the final yard of the field was left until the Corn Mother, in her terrible aspect of winter, had been driven away by being beaten out by the reapers, after which it was cut by an old woman. Alternatively, if the last stalks embodied the goddess in her more benevolent and youthful aspects, they were gathered and tied with ribbon, and the sheaf was placed reverentially in the barn where she remained to oversee the threshing. This final cut, sometimes called The Maiden, was often reaped by the youngest girl among the workers in the field. In other traditions the procedure involved weighting the centre of the last sheaf with stones before it was carried home to make it seem as if a body was contained within it. It is this belief in the presence of the Corn Mother that has underpinned the fashioning of Corn Dollies and other images which represent the goddess as the Corn Baby or the Corn Maiden and which are kept to ensure fertility in the following year until the next crop is harvested.

Pagan traditions have maintained that the person who cuts the last of the field is the host into which the dying Corn Spirit flees. He thus becomes the human representative of the deity and must be sacrificed in order to ensure the fertility of the crop in the following year. This ancient ritual of slaughter gave rise in English country lore to the figure of John Barleycorn, the reaper of the last stand, who was symbolically put to death at harvest time, embodying the dying god of summer and plenty. In other traditions the Corn Spirit has been seen to escape into various animal representatives, including oxen, dogs, cats and cockerels.

Woad (*Isatis tinctoria*)

Where and when

Although not indigenous to Europe, the plant has been extensively cultivated over many centuries, and is naturalized on waste ground and other poor soils in various places as far north as Sweden. In the British Isles it grows truly wild only at Tewkesbury near Gloucester and at Guildford. Elsewhere it has to be classed as a casual. It flowers from June to August.

Appearance

An annual or biennial growing 60–100 cm (2–3 ft) high, the lower leaves are lance-shaped, greyish and downy, coarsely toothed and stalked; the upper ones clasp the stem and are hairless. The flowers are small and yellow with four petals, and the fruit is a pod which hangs down (unusually among the cabbage group) and which ripens to a shining dark brown. Woad is a member of the Cruciferae family.

Traditions and associations

One of the chief reasons for cultivation of Woad lay in the extraction of a permanent blue dye from its leaves. Although little is known of the circumstances, the colorant is thought to have been used extensively by the ancient Britons as a body paint, which they believed held magical properties and would protect them in battle. The use of this dye may have been made even more dramatic if a report by the Roman writer Polybius is anything to go by. He reports Gaulish troops at Telamon, whom he refers to as the *Gaesatae*, going into battle naked. This seems to have been an archaic tradition among the Celts, which died out in the later period of their hegemony.

Woad was once extensively cultivated around Toulouse in France, but, as a source of dye, it has largely been superseded by indigo.

Wood Sorrel *(Oxalis acetosella)*

Where and when

Abundant in woodlands throughout Europe, the British Isles and much of western and central Asia, the Wood Sorrel is also indigenous to North America. It flowers in the early spring. This plant is probably the original later emulated by the Irish Shamrock.

Appearance

A small, low-growing plant with delicate, pretty flowers. The green parts arise from a slender rootstock. On casual inspection the flower is not unlike that of the Wood Anemone (*Anemone nemorosa*). There is a basal rosette of leaves with long stalks and trifoliate, rounded-ovate leaflets.

The flowers are borne on long, slender stalks and bear five large, white, pinkish or purple-tinged petals. The foliage has a mildly acid taste.

Traditions and associations

Many plants which bear trifoliate leaves have taken on strong religious significance, being seen to represent the Trinity. The Shamrock was no exception, having been allegedly the means by which St Patrick illustrated the principle of Father, Son and Holy Ghost. Subsequently it became the national emblem of Ireland and is still worn, by tradition, in buttonholes on St Patrick's Day, 17 March. The mystic associations of Wood Sorrel predate Christianity, however, since the plant was sacred to the pagan Celts, the Druids revering it for its magical properties. In later centuries, the medieval herbalists considered the plant highly therapeutic in combating fevers and reducing bodily inflammations. The English herbalist Gerard notes: 'When stamped and used for greene sauce, it is good for them that have sicke and feeble stomackes; for it strengtheneth the stomacke and procureth appetite.' Because of the signature of its leaves, 'broad at the ends, cut in the middle and sharp towards the stalk', Wood Sorrel was also considered beneficial as a treatment of heart disease.

It came to be known among monastic orders as the Hallelujah Plant, and evidence of its appeal in non-secular life is to be found in a number of old churches where its trefoil shape can sometimes be found among the roof carving motifs.

Also known as Cuckowes Meat and Wood Sour, this little plant was said by some of the old apothecaries to benefit the cuckoo, because 'either the cuckoo feedeth thereon, or by reason when it springeth forth and flowereth the cuckoo singeth most'. In country districts, before the introduction to Britain of the more substantial French Sorrel in about 1596, the tangy, slightly acid flavour of Wood Sorrel made it popular as a potherb cooked like spinach.

Yarrow *(Achillea millefolium)*

Where and when

A common weed, growing in an assortment of grassy places and frequently seen in garden lawns. Found across temperate Europe and large parts of North America, Yarrow flowers throughout the summer.

Appearance

A dark green perennial growing up to 50 cm (20 in), tall with a toughish stem, and bearing very finely cut, dark green leaves on short branches. The plant spreads by creeping runners. The leaves and stems are downy and above-ground parts are aromatic. The small, white flowers are borne in flattish umbels.

Traditions and associations

One of the earliest links known to archaeology between plants and the supernatural was found in 1960 in the highlands of northern Iraq, where a Neanderthal flower burial was discovered that was proved by radiocarbon-dating to be not less than 60,000 years old. Among the pollen grains that were found in close proximity to one of the bodies, buried some 6 m (20 ft) below the present-day level of the cave floor, were clumps of Yarrow pollen. In such clumped formation it was established that the pollen could not have drifted in on air currents, and therefore must have come from flowers placed on or around the corpse. Yarrow, in common with other flowers left at the same time, has been known from ancient times as a healing herb, being particularly effective in the curing of wounds. Was this therefore some arcane warrior who had perished in battle? We will never know, but it is clear that these Neanderthal people had probably discovered the benefits of this inconspicuous member of the Daisy family (Compositae) when they laid an unrecorded member of their tribe in his last resting place and prepared him for the journey to the next world.

During the Classical era, Yarrow was better known as Militaris, and was valued for its healing properties. Tradition grew up linking it with Achilles who, it was said, had learned of its mysterious powers from the physician Centaur, Chiron. It was the latter who treated Achilles for the burns inflicted by his mother when she tried to incinerate him as her unlucky seventh child.

Yarrow has also been a respected herb in the arts of divination and witchcraft. In this context it is generally accepted that it must be cut on the night of the full moon to be effective. Yarrow has generally acquired a poor reputation, though, and has been called Mother-die and Fever-plant, unlucky if brought into the house, where it was thought to cause sickness.

One of the more curious applications, which may possess elements of contradictory truth, has been to stem or to encourage nosebleeds. According to Lightfoot's *Flora Scotica* of 1777: 'The common people in order to cure the Headache do sometimes thrust a leaf of it up their nostrils, to make their nose bleed.'

The *Folk Lore Record* of 1878 includes a similar observation in a rhyme which was recited by young girls in love:

Green 'arrow, green 'arrow, you wears a white bow;
If my love love me, my nose will bleed now;
If my love don't love me, it 'ont bleed a drop;
If my love do love me, 'twill bleed every drop.

PART TWO

Trees

P A R T 2

Trees

Introduction

THERE EXISTS A mystical power to trees, a vast spiritual strength by which many of us feel drawn to them. To walk in a great forest is to enter a living thing filled with immense mystery and depth, and it would be a rare individual who did not occasionally feel a spine-pricking tug as they followed a lonely woodland path through the gathering shadows of evening. The scattered vestiges of woodland that we see dotting the landscape today, however, are nothing compared with the seemingly endless forests that confronted our ancestors. In Roman times, north of the Danube, the Hercynian Forest extended eastwards from the Rhine and probably seemed truly unfathomable. Much of western Europe and the British Isles were similarly clothed, and so trees dominated people's lives. They represented the largest and most indomitable of all living things and many of them, outstripping as they did the human span of life, seemed both immortal and indestructible.

Thus there is seen to be an immanence about such mighty entities, and they are more than mere tangible living things. They possess a cryptic power which singles them out over all other objects in nature for a special kind of holiness. Their trunks reach upwards from roots that penetrate deep within the womb of the earth, while their topmost branches touch the sky and the heavens. Coated with the rime of winter, many of them take on a spectral appearance. The Ash, one of the most sacred of trees, can adopt fantastic and distorted shapes in old age when parts of it die away and leave gnarled bare arms rising starkly against the skyline. A conifer surges upwards with cathedral-like serenity, while a Birch in the early months of spring takes on a virginal fluttery shyness that earns it the title of the Lady of the Woods.

It is not surprising that, in times gone by, the great woods became sanctified. Tacitus, speaking of the Celts living beyond the civilized extremities of the Roman Empire, wrote: 'They deem it incompatible with the majesty of the heavenly host to confine the gods within walls, or to mould them into any likeness of the human face; they consecrate groves and coppices, and they give the divine names to that mysterious something which is visible only to the eyes of faith.' Thus the priests of these sylvan 'cathedrals' created their hallowed groves or sanctuaries, secret clearings or glades, deep in the forests, perhaps marked by little more than a circle of stones. In this they were paralleled by the Greeks and Romans with their sacred 'temenos' (groves).

The Celts may have developed a whole secret subculture based on trees. A curious work entitled *Cad Goddeu* ('The Battle of the Trees') has been attributed to the sixth-century Welsh poet Taliesin, and it relates what may have been an important religious event in the Druidic year in Britain, a symbolic battle between the forces of nature. Robert Graves bases much of *The White Goddess* on the Taliesin poems and suggests that the names of the trees were used to develop an esoteric alphabet which was transmitted on the fingers in similar manner to a deaf-and-dumb sign language. The mechanism of this alphabet, known as Beth-Luis-Nion after the first three Celtic tree names, the equivalents of Birch, Rowan and Ash, has been explained by Roderick O'Flaherty in his book *Ogygia,* the title of which is drawn from the mythical Greek island of the same name on which Odysseus was held captive by the goddess, Calypso.

The sacred quality attached to trees has had various spin-offs. It has made their felling a significant act and, from the Bronze Age onwards the axe, which began its existence not as a weapon of war but as a working tool, also took on a spiritual dimension. The axe came to possess a paradoxical significance both as an agent of death and as a fertility symbol, because out of the decomposition of the felled tree were seen to spring the saplings of regeneration. Not least because of the longevity of trees, which in many cases may equal or extend beyond that of the human life span, the wellbeing of a particular tree has often been linked to the prosperity of an individual. If the tree becomes sickly or suffers damage, it bodes badly for its owner, but the association can go even further. Much of John Steinbeck's fine novel, *To A God Unknown*, which examines traditions among farming settlers in California, is based on reverence for an ancient Oak tree in which the central character, Joseph Wayne, believes that the spirit of his father resides. As he says to a young Mexican boy: 'My father is in that tree. My father is that tree!'

We are, in many respects, no less committed to the sacred nature of trees now than were the ancient Irish Celts with their holy 'bile' trees. The Robin Hood Oak in Sherwood Forest is seen, in some senses, as the living representation of an English folk hero. The Glastonbury Thorn is treasured and its cuttings nurtured with all the diligence of tending a holy relic. Scores of protesters go to extreme lengths to save trees which stand in the way of road developments.

The Rowan is considered to be one of the most magical trees and is important in witchcraft.

Once, many years ago, when attending a midsummer service in the chapel at Brighton College, I listened to an Anglican bishop offering his young congregation some memorable, if unusual advice. They were to go and put their arms around the most ancient tree they could find, and to shut their eyes, and to wait. He promised that something remarkable would happen – an energy would flow from the tree to the person, like electricity.

Most trees, in one sense or another, possess magical and mysterious colours. Those included here are only the most important among many.

Alder *(Alnus glutinosa)*

Where and when

Common throughout Europe and western Asia as far north as the edge of the Arctic Circle, Alder occurs in wet woods and water meadows, and along the banks of streams where it flowers in the early spring before the leaves have emerged. In size it can range from a small shrub to a comparatively tall tree.

Appearance

A deciduous species with darkish foliage of stalked, broadly ovate and sharply toothed leaves, Alder is a member of the Birch family (Betulaceae). The flowers are borne separately, the yellowish male catkins being produced in the autumn, in drooping clusters of two or three, the purplish female catkins of spring being shorter, erect and more ovoid in shape. In the spring months, these catkins may, from a distance, give the tree a purplish appearance. Outwardly, the fruits are not dissimilar to a small fircone, and they may frequently persist on the branches.

Traditions and associations

The Celtic words for Alder include *bran* and *fearn*, and Bran was the eponymous heroic god of mythical tales in both the Welsh and Irish traditions. In the *Mabinogion*, Gwydion guesses the name of Bran because he carries Alder twigs in his hand, and Bran has long been regarded as the god of the Alder. Fearn is the name given to the fourth letter in the Beth-Luis-Nion tree alphabet which Robert Graves claims was used by the Druids. In this he echoes the assumption contained in Roderick O'Flaherty's *Ogygia*.

In the Celtic saga of the Battle of the Trees, the *Cad Goddeu* from the *Romance of Taliesin*, in which the protagonists are Arawn on the one side and the sons of Don, Gwydion and Amathaon on the other, the Alder is in the front line of combatants. It is described as one of the 'hottest of the trees', probably because its charcoal produces an intense heat, although, in the fateful outcome, Bran's Alder is vanquished by Gwydion's Ash. In some derivative versions of the Classical legend of the death of Heracles (Hercules) the hero is cremated on an Alder-wood pyre at the midsummer solstice, and his immolated remains are floated away down a river on an Alder-wood boat.

The association of Alder with fire is reinforced by the fact that it is very resistant to decomposition in water, and has been widely used to construct aqueducts and building foundations in marshy areas and places liable to flooding. Many of the very earliest houses discovered in the archaeology of Europe, which were sited on the margins of lakes, were built on Alder piles. It was also employed traditionally in the manufacture of buckets used to carry liquids such as water and milk, and it has been a source of some valuable dyes in bygone times. The bark especially was processed to extract a fine red colorant, a factor which adds to the already strong association with fire.

Almond *(Prunus amygdalus)*

Where and when

Related to the Apricot and Peach, the Almond, from the Mediterranean region, has become extensively cultivated as an ornamental, and is now naturalized across much of Europe and Asia.

Appearance

A smallish tree with undivided, toothed, ovate leaves. The flowers are showy, pink, lilac or white and appear early in spring before the leaves. The fruit is the familiar nut surrounded by a soft green epicarp.

Traditions and associations

According to the tragedy of Attis and Kybele, best known from Greek and Roman literature, but whose Phrygian cult originated in Anatolia, the vegetation deity Attis was conceived miraculously when his mother, Nana, placed a ripe Almond fruit in her bosom.

In ancient Phrygia the Almond was regarded as the father of all things, perhaps because its blossom is among the first to appear in spring before the leaves have sprouted on the tree. The Almond is also the tree from which, according to apocryphal sources, Moses' successor, Aaron, cut his staff. The Jewish *menorah* candlestick is thus said to represent the Almond staff after it has sprouted seven branches, and its sconces are traditionally modelled on Almond fruits. In the Christian era, the tree in blossom has been assigned, in various Catholic countries including Spain and Italy, to the Virgin Mary.

The strictly pagan fertility connotations have continued. During the nineteenth century, in Germany, a custom prevailed to present a bride and groom with Almonds at their wedding banquet, while in Czechoslovakia it was customary to distribute sprigs of Almond among the wedding guests.

In a distinct tradition, eating Almonds is believed to be divinatory. It presages a journey, successful or otherwise, the outcome depending on whether the Almond is sweet or bitter.

Apple *(Pyrus malus)*

Where and when

All the cultivated varieties of Apple grown in orchards have been developed from the original wild species, which still grows in woods and hedgerows all over Europe and western Asia, extending northwards into parts of Scandinavia. It flowers in spring.

Appearance

A smallish, spreading tree with ovate, finely toothed leaves that are downy on the underside. The distinctive flowers, either wholly white or with a pinkish tinge, are arranged in short-stalked racemes. The fruits of the wild Crab Apple are small, acrid pomes which appear green when young and take on a reddish tint when ripe.

Traditions and associations

'And when the woman saw that the tree was good for food and that it was pleasant to the eyes, and a tree to be desired to make one wise, she took of the fruit thereof, and did eat, and gave also unto her husband with her; and he did eat.' Thus, according to Genesis 3.6, did the curtain come down on Paradise, but how this anonymously fruiting instrument of the Fall came to be identified as the humble Apple is unclear, though its reputation is certainly apocryphal.

The Apple was already an object of magical significance to the Greeks. Mythology has it that the Golden Apples of the Hesperides grew in the extreme west 'beyond the ocean' at the foot of Mount Atlas on the so-called Islands of the Blessed. A gift from the earth goddess, Gaia, given to Hera on the occasion of her marriage to Zeus and clearly possessing magical significance, the Apples were tended by the Nymphs of the Setting Sun, the three daughters of Nyx – Aegle (Brightness), Erythia (Scarlet) and Hesperarethusa (Sunset Glow) – who guarded them against all comers, particularly the daughters of Atlas who were not averse to occasional Apple scrumping, with the help of a dragon, the offspring of Typhon and Echidna. The future of the orchard appeared secure until the hero Heracles (Hercules) was given the task of collecting the Golden Apples as part of his labours at the bidding of Eurystheus. Having travelled far and encountered numerous antagonists *en route*, Heracles learned that the only person who could obtain the Apples was the giant, Atlas, who was preoccupied with supporting the world. Heracles persuaded Atlas to obtain three of the Golden Apples in return for having the weight of the sky taken from his shoulders for a while. When Atlas returned with the trophy, he offered to take it to Eurystheus personally, but Heracles was equal to the ruse which would have left him carrying Atlas' unwelcome burden. He asked the giant to take the weight for a moment while he shifted it to a more comfortable position but as soon as Atlas was holding the vault of heaven once more, Heracles picked up the Apples and made his timely escape. At least one of the accounts of the saga has Eurystheus at a loss to know what to do with the Golden Apples, so he returns them to Heracles who gallantly presents them to Athena. She elects to return them to the Hesperides and the story ends happily for all.

Norse mythology also includes an account of sacred Apples which possess the secret of eternal youth and are tended by the goddess Idunn, the wife of Bragi, for the daily consumption of the Aesir gods and goddesses of Asgard. There is some argument that this northern European tale represents a case of literary borrowing and adaptation of the Greek story. In the *Haustlong* saga, which is summarized by Snorri Sturluson in the *Prose Edda*, the Machiavellian demigod Loki is persuaded to abduct Idunn and her Apples for the benefit of the giant Thiassi upon which the disgruntled deities with Othin at their head, deprived of their regular elixir, begin to age with considerable rapidity. Their *status quo* is only restored when Loki is coerced into bring Idunn and her vital cargo back to Asgard. Richard Wagner makes much of the plot in his opera *Das Rheingold,* though he transposes the somewhat anonymous figure of Idunn for the better-known fertility goddess Freya, and has her removed from Valhalla in compensation to the giant builders of the fortress. She is returned only when the illicitly obtained gold of the Rhinemaidens is forfeited in payment, an ill-fated contract which presages the ultimate downfall of the illustrious gods.

The fertility connotation has been retained and, in more recent times, Frazer records that barren women in the region of Kirghizstan roll themselves on the ground under a solitary Apple tree in order to become pregnant. In some parts of Europe it has also been customary to plant an Apple tree at the birth of a male child, the health of the tree being an indicator of the health of the person throughout his life. In many areas of Europe which came under the Celtic star, Apples have been imbued with a special sacred significance as the bearers of a life-giving fruit and in Wales they have been viewed as the 'noblest of trees'. Apples were being cultivated Britain from about 3000 BC and, because of the potency of the drink produced from their fermentation, they may have been linked with orgiastic rites.

In the west of England, particularly in Somerset where the cider industry is strongest, there persist powerful traditions associated with the Apple, and the name Avalon is said to mean 'The Place of Apples'. The wassailing tradition is still maintained, usually taking place on Twelfth Night when cakes are placed in the trees and cider is thrown at the trees as a libation to the spirits. This has been accompanied by the firing of guns and the banging of pots and pans to drive evil spirits from the orchard and ensure a good crop in the coming season. The ritual is accompanied by the Wassail Song.

Strong cider is popularly referred to as the Witches' Brew and the night of Hallowe'en has

been associated with Apple rituals in many counties of England. Witches revere it as a fruit since the Apple, when sliced open, reveals the magical symbol of the five-pointed star or pentagram. In Lancashire there was a tradition known as Duck Apple Night when pieces of Apple were floated in a bowl of water and children had to duck their heads to bite them. Whole Apples were also hung on strings with the same objective in mind and all these games were considered to bring luck to those who managed to eat the fruit. In medical lore there has existed a quack country remedy, known especially from the Westphalian region of Germany, which believes that an Apple, crushed and mixed with saffron, will keep jaundice at bay. Whether such popular remedies had any remedial basis or not we still retain, in common English usage, the old saying: 'An apple a day keeps the doctor away.'

Ash, Common *(Fraxinus excelsior)*

Where and when

This tall and elegant deciduous tree is one of a small number of related species all of which are limited more or less to the temperate regions of the northern hemisphere. Favouring chalk and limestone soils, it is common in woodlands throughout most of Britain, though it thins out in northern parts of Scotland and in Scandinavia where the climate becomes too cold. It is replaced by a similar, though distinct, species in Mediterranean regions.

Appearance

The flowers appear before the leaves in spring, as clusters of purplish-black stamens surrounded by a few small, woolly scales. These ripen later in the season to produce winged capsules known as 'keys'. The winter buds are black and somewhat angular and the leaves are borne in opposite pinnate arrangement, each consisting of between 7 and 11 lance-shaped toothed leaflets. The bark is at first smooth and grey, gradually becoming more roughened with age. The Ash is a member of the Olive family (Oleaceae).

Traditions and associations

The Ash, perhaps more than any other tree, has been afforded a special mystique since very early times. Among the first references to its more esoteric character the Greek writer, Hesiod (*Works and Days*), mentions that the Ash is possessed by malevolent nymphs known as the Meliae, and the Greeks also made the Ash sacred to the sea god, Poseidon, in his alternative role as Husband of the Earth. In Germanic and Norse cultures the Ash has been regarded as a sacred tree, the World Tree or Yggdrasil, and it is traditionally associated with the father of the gods, Woden or Othin. The term Yggdrasil is a curious one which stands, literally translated, as the 'horse of Othin', but that expression possesses sinister connotations and means, in effect, a gallows tree, since it was from Yggdrasil that the god hanged himself in the pursuit of eternal knowledge.

I wot that I hung on the wind-tossed tree
of all nights nine,
wounded by spear, bespoken to Othin
bespoken myself to myself,
upon that tree of which nine telleth
from what roots it doth rise.

(After the 'rune poem' of the *Havamal* of the *Poetic Edda*)

The tree is described by Snorri Sturluson (*Prose Edda*) during the tale of Gylfi's quest for answers to the mysteries of life: The Ash is of all trees the biggest and best. Its branches spread out over all the world and across the sky. Three of the roots support it and extend a very, very long way. One is among the Aesir (the gods), the second is among the frost giants, where Ginnungagap once was. The third extends over Niflheim (the underworld), and under that root is Hvergelmir, and Nithogg (a huge predacious worm) gnaws the bottom of the root.

It seems evident that, in Viking culture, the tree was believed to possess life-giving properties, with its fruit perhaps offering strength to women in pregnancy or labour. Yet it has also been seen to retain a forbidden strength, much as the Tree of the Biblical Genesis saga, which will only be revealed at the end of the existing order. In the *Poetic Edda*, the *Fjolsvinnsmal* includes the following obscure lines:

Tell me, Fjolsvith, for fain I would know;
answer thou as I ask:
of the fruit what becomes of that far spreading tree,
since nor fire nor iron will fell it?
Of its berries thou shalt bear on fire,
for ailing women to eat:
then out will come what within was held –
such strength is bestowed on that tree.

The Yggdrasil is part of the framework of Creation, its branches spreading over earth and heaven and its roots creating a ladder between worlds. It is the guardian of the ordered world and so its doom, and that of the gods whose destinies it watches over, are inseparably linked. In Norse religion the world of the gods is destined to come crashing down on the day of doom, Ragnarok, as the final battle with the frost giants takes its terrible toll. The World Ash, while destined to be swept up in the all-consuming fires, is integral to this moment of apocalypse, and it is clear from other Norse poetry that within its trunk shelter the two human beings who will begin the new earth after Ragnarok. The *Voluspa* tells of its end in chilling words of prophecy:

Mimirs's sons dance; the downfall bodes
when blares the gleaming old Gjallarhorn;
loud blows Heimdall, with horn aloft;
In Hel's dark hall horror spreadeth,
once more Othin with Mimir's head (wisdom) speaketh
ere Surt's sibling (fire) swallows him.
Trembles the towering tree Yggdrasil.
its leaves sough loudly; unleashed is the giant.

(Translation by Lee M. Hollander)

According to Robert Graves, the Ash was also sacred to the Welsh Celtic god and hero, Gwion, and in the *Cad Goddeu* ('Battle of the Trees') it is described as the 'cruel and gloomy ash'. It is also listed as the third tree, Nion, of the magical tree alphabet known as the Beth-Luis-Nion, and described in Roderick O'Flaherty's *Ogygia*.

The Ash has been regarded as a lucky tree. In Cornwall an old tradition has it that plucking an ash leaf brings a boon:

Even ash, I do thee pluck,
Hoping thus to meet good luck.
If no luck I get from thee
I shall wish thee on the tree.

Among the more recent associated traditions, it is recorded by several authors that children suffering from the common Victorian complaints of rupture and rickets would be passed through a cleft in an Ash trunk either before sunrise, or 'against the sun'. A young sapling would be split down part of its length and the naked child passed backwards and forwards several times. The tree was then bound up tightly and its wound covered with clay or mud. In subsequent years these trees were watched over diligently by those who had been passed through their fissures, since it was believed that the life of the patient and the life of the tree were inextricably bound together. The best publicized of these grew in a street in Solihull and was the subject of an engraving in the *Gentleman's Magazine* of May 1804.

In various parts of England the carrying of Ash leaves on which the leaflets were in even number was considered to provide a talisman. An Ash stick was regarded as the best safeguard against snake bites, and Frazer in *The Golden Bough* describes an old Cheshire remedy for warts, in which they are rubbed with a slice of bacon which is then inserted beneath the young bark of an Ash. The warts disappear from the hand but, in the course of time, reappear as rough patches on the tree bark. Alternatively, the wart could be pressed with a pin, which was then stuck into the tree bark. These traditions are no more than vestiges of ancient sympathetic magic. On the negative side, the failure of the Ash-seed crop was believed to foretell disaster. In this respect a particularly bad season was recorded prior to the execution of Charles I! The Ash has even been a source of springtime weather forecasting in the familiar rhyme: 'If the Ash before the Oak, we shall surely get a soak; If the Oak before the Ash, we shall only get a splash.'

The Ash has also been closely associated with European witchcraft, and its magical properties have made it a dangerous tree to fell. The witch's *stang* or stave is traditionally cut from an Ash stem, as is the haft of the besom broom. In parts of Lincolnshire, however, a good length of Ash was regarded as a defence against the powers of a witch.

Birch *(Betula alba)*

Where and when

One of the oldest re-colonizers of the European continent as the last Ice Age receded northwards, this graceful tree is found growing chiefly on sandy and gravelly soils and is widespread and common in woodlands and shrubby heaths. In Scotland and other northern regions, it is largely replaced by the Downy Birch (*Betula pubescens*) but the Birches extend throughout the northern hemisphere.

Appearance

Never growing to any great size, and often, in northern regions, remaining shrubby, the Birch possesses distinctive pendulous branches and peeling, white bark which becomes roughened and cracked towards the base of the trunk. The flowers appear in spring, male catkins are long, extending up to 5 cm (2 in), while the female flowers are shorter and more compact. The leaves are alternate, ovate, taper-pointed and toothed, tending, because of their slender stalks, to tremble in the breeze, like those of Aspen (*Populus tremula*).

Traditions and associations

Known as the Lady of the Woods, the Birch has invariably taken on female attributes, because of its delicate tracery of leaves and its trembling habit. It has been the object of numerous spring fertility rites, probably because it is generally the first tree to put out new shoots in the spring. In Russia there has existed a tradition in which, on the Thursday before Whitsun, villagers go out into the woods and chop down a Birch sapling, which they then dress in women's clothes and deck with ribbons in honour of the tree spirit. After a feast, the decked and garlanded tree is carried to the house of a villager where it stays as an honoured guest until Whitsun, after which it is hurled into a river. Elsewhere in Russia, a parallel rite has been conducted, in which a maiden is dressed in young Birch boughs and carried around the village. Bunches of Birch twigs, their buds bursting, have also been carried around as part of traditional Mayday celebrations in parts of Scandinavia. Elsewhere in Europe, Birch boughs have been essential equipment in the ceremony of Beating the Bounds, and they are generally regarded as efficacious in driving out inclement spirits. A bundle of birch twigs has been traditionally applied to the haft of a besom broom, beloved of witches. It has certainly been considered a lucky tree and, in this context, sweethearts would sometimes give a sprig of Birch to their lovers. It also provided a traditional wood for making infants' cradles.

The Birch, or *Beth*, constitutes the first letter of the Beth-Luis-Nion tree alphabet, claimed to be of ancient Druidic origin and described by Robert Graves from the book by Roderick O'Flaherty, *Ogygia*, and as such represents the first month of the year after the winter solstice.

Blackthorn *(Prunus spinosa)*

Where and when

Common throughout Europe and northern Asia, and particularly plentiful in the British Isles where it grows in open woodlands, hedges and thickets, it is the original derivation of the cultivated Damson and Plum. Blackthorn is one of the first of the hedgerow trees to blossom.

Appearance

A shrub with a stiff widely branching habit, the stems characteristically blackish in colour and armed with sharp thorns. The leaves are ovate, smooth and very finely toothed. The small, white flowers are produced in short spikes before the leaves in early spring, maturing into the purplish 'sloe' fruits, which frequently have a bluish bloom until picked. The fruit has an intensely sharp and astringent taste.

Tradition and associations

In company with May, the Blackthorn has been regarded as a particularly unlucky plant to bring indoors when it blooms in April and May. Like the Holy Thorn, it was reputed to bloom on the Old Christmas Day which fell on 6 January, before the calendar revisions of 1752 removed 11 days, in losing the Julian and adopting the Continental Gregorian year. The notion of ill luck had Christian associations since it was the Blackthorn even more than the Hawthorn from which, tradition had it, that the Crown of Thorns of the Passion was made. It was also believed, erroneously, that the May, or Whitethorn, will destroy a Blackthorn growing nearby.

Known in Old English as the *Straif*, Blackthorn has been widely associated with witchcraft and with blasting (striking another person or object with an imprecation or curse). Graves describes the fear in which someone walking with a 'black rod' of Blackthorn was held in parts of the west of England, since the practice marked them out as a witch. In reality a blasting rod was a wand or stave made out of more or less any material hard enough to be durable and effective as an occasional weapon, but Blackthorn, with its dark connotations, became popular in the eyes of the Church as a witch's tool. It is reported that when the Covenanter and self-confessed witch, Major Weir, was burnt at the stake in 1670 in Edinburgh, his Blackthorn rod was consigned to the flames with him Its reputation was particularly strong in the Midlands and the industrial northwest, and a number of English villages have links with this practice, including Blackrod near Bolton in Lancashire. The Usher of the House of Lords and the Order of the Garter is also so called because of his tradition of knocking on the doors of Parliament at its opening and proroguing with a Blackthorn rod.

In Surrey, one finds the witness to Blackthorn's early blossoming in an old proverb: 'It's always cold when the Blackthorn comes into flower.'

Elder *(Sambucus nigra)*

Where and when

A very common small tree or shrub which extends through Europe as far as the Caucasus, surviving as a cultivated introduction in more northerly regions. Preferring chalky soils, it appears in woods, thickets and waste places where it readily takes a foothold. Elder belongs to the Honeysuckle family (Caprifoliaceae).

Appearance

Britain's only native shrub to bear opposite, pinnate leaves, each with five broadly lance-shaped leaflets. The stems tend to be brittle with a distinctive white pith, and the bark is fissured and corky. The flowers appear in June and July and consist of broad, flattened umbels of small, creamy white flowers with pale yellow anthers. The clusters of small round fruits, green at first, ripen to purplish-black and are edible. All parts have a rather distinctive and somewhat unpleasant odour to them.

Traditions and associations

Much of the mystique of this tree stems from the wholly apocryphal idea stemming from Langland's tale of *Piers Plowman* that Judas, the disciple that betrayed Jesus Christ to the Roman authorities, hanged himself from an Elder tree. The Acts of the Apostles, conversely, states that Judas purchased a field, tripped and fell headlong, splitting himself open and losing his bowels. The myth has been aided and abetted by the year-round appearance on the boughs of Elder of the curiously shaped Jew's Ear fungus (*Auricularia auricula-judae*) which selectively, though not exclusively, uses the tree as a host. Elder has also been described as the tree of the Crucifixion, though again there is no Biblical support for the idea. In the Beth-Luis-Nion tree alphabet, claimed to derive from Druidic practices and described by Roderick O'Flaherty in *Ogygia*, it is Ruis, the tree of the thirteenth month.

From these notions Elder has been cast as an unlucky tree, having been associated with the more malevolent aspects of witchcraft and as a bringer of doom. Many countrymen still regard the cutting of Elder in a hedgerow as a portent of ill luck, and burning Elder wood in the hearth is said to 'bring the Devil into the house'. It was considered particularly foolhardy to make an infant's cradle from Elder wood, the child being sure to be pinched black and blue by the Elder Mother who lived in it.

In apparent contradiction, the burning of Elder wood is said to reveal the presence of witches in the neighbourhood, while an Elder planted near the house will keep witches at bay. There was a time when an Elder tree could be found growing beside the back door of most country cottages, not merely as a protection against witchcraft but also because of the belief that a house thus protected will never be struck by lightning. As with some other trees, Elder was also believed to provide a quack cure for warts if the warts were touched with a pin, and this was then inserted into a length of the bough which was buried and left to rot.

In March 1966 an article in the *Brighton Evening Argus* reported that a bizarre though anonymous notice of cursing had been pinned to the trunk of an aged Elder tree at Steyning in Sussex, directed at whoever might fell it. The tree stood in the way of a housing development at Steyning.

Elderflower wine has, since time immemorial, been considered an excellent tonic, and in days gone by the extracted juice was taken as an anti-emetic treatment and as a country cure for the dropsy.

It should be added that the Elder possesses a magic of an altogether different kind for every small boy living in country districts, as the raw material of the original pea-shooter! As Culpeper puts it: 'I hold it needless to write any description of this, since every boy that plays with a pop-gun will not mistake another tree instead of the elder.'

Hawthorn *(Crataegus monogyna)*

Where and when

Also commonly known as May, this generally small thorny tree occurs throughout much of Europe and Asia except in the far north. In the British Isles and elsewhere it is much cultivated as a stockproof hedging. It blossoms, as the name suggests, in May and early June, although it may produce a second, later flowering.

Appearance

Most commonly growing as a shrub, but sometimes developing into a larger tree, the Hawthorn has stems armed with sharp stout thorns. The leaves are deeply lobed and the white or pinkish flowers develop in broad, strongly scented umbels. The fruit, known as a 'haw', is a small berry containing a single 'stone' and is dull red in colour.

Traditions and associations

The Hawthorn is a tree which has been regarded as being of great magical and religious significance. During the first century AD, according to tradition, St Joseph of Arimathaea visited Glastonbury in his capacity as a tin trader, possibly accompanied by the child Jesus. Following the Crucifixion and sometime after AD 37, he returned, made contact with Druids at Glastonbury and, while there, thrust his staff into the ground at the foot of Wearyall Hill where it promptly took root and burst into leaf. This event was considered miraculous in itself but it was then established that the Holy Thorn, as it came to be known, blossomed twice a year, in springtime and at the old date of Christmas, 6 January, before the reform of the Julian calendar to fall in with the Continental Gregorian system. The Glastonbury Thorn is said occasionally to show simultaneous evidence of buds, flowers, berries and dead leaves.

Successive generations of the Holy Thorn have, of course, been propagated down the centuries, and grafts have been sent all over the world to grow in such places as Central Park, New York. Each year at Christmas, sprays of the blossom are cut by the Mayor of Glastonbury and delivered to the Queen's breakfast table in a tradition which is said to have begun in the reign of Queen Anne.

The destruction of a Hawthorn was always considered a perilous operation, and during the Cromwellian Interregnum a fanatical Puritan is claimed to have attempted to chop the original Glastonbury tree down, but only succeeded in partly severing the trunk. He was rewarded, so the story goes, with a splinter which struck him in the eye and resulted in blindness. Others who have tried to damage Holy Thorns have suffered similar ill luck. In the nineteenth-century *Folklore of the British Isles* by E. M. Hull, instances are cited involving the death of children or cattle and the loss of money. A Worcestershire farmer who felled one reputedly suffered a broken leg and a disastrous fire shortly thereafter, and there are many similar tales of misfortune.

Other ancient Hawthorns have enjoyed different mystical reputations. One that has stood near the church in the village of Hethel near Norwich in Norfolk and is protected by the Norfolk Trust is claimed to be many centuries old, and is popularly known as the Witch of Hethel. There is said to be a deed in existence dated to the early part of the thirteenth century stating that this Hawthorn tree was 'old' even at that time.

In The *White Goddess*, Robert Graves observes that Welsh mythology has the Hawthorn appear as the malevolent Chief of the Giants, Yspaddaden Penkawr.

The Hawthorn is given strangely contradictory attributes, and generally it has been regarded as an unlucky tree, but all its esoteric associations, good and bad, can probably be traced back as relics of ancient tree worship. In many parts of the British Isles, to bring May blossom into the house is considered highly dangerous, and even greater risk is attached to sleeping in a room with May. On the other hand, there have been widespread traditions of young Mayday revellers bringing back May boughs, using them to decorate doorways, and Frazer quotes an old rhyme:

We've been rambling all the night/
and sometime of this day
And now, returning back again,/
we bring a garland gay
A garland gay we bring you here/
and at your door we stand
It is a sprout well budded out,/
the work of our Lord's hand.

There was an old Suffolk tradition by which any farm labourer who brought in May in bloom on Mayday was rewarded, while in Staffordshire branches of May placed in the attic would safeguard the house from witchcraft and other mayhem. In some parts of the country, to sit under a Hawthorn brings misfortune but in others luck, and to bathe in the dew beneath a Hawthorn on Mayday morning was rumoured to be a guaranteed beauty treatment. In Lincolnshire, the young springtime leaves and shoots used to be popular with children as a free hedgerow snack, known as 'bread and cheese'. In parts of Scotland the tree has been regarded as a weather vane, an abundance of fruit foretelling a hard winter ahead: 'Many haws, many snaws.'

The tree has been provided with strongly sexual connotations chiefly through the traditions of the maypole and its attendant spring fertility dances. The witch's stang or stave, itself a male symbol, has also been garlanded, by convention, with May for the spring Sabbat festival of Beltane. Hawthorn has, however, not infrequently operated as a botanical chastity belt, separating amorous swains, at least for a time, from the virginal objects of their desire, the German fairy tale of *Sleeping Beauty* providing the most celebrated of such roles.

Hazel *(Corylus avellana)*

Where and when

Common throughout the temperate regions of the northern hemisphere, Hazel grows in woods, hedgerows, thickets and waste places, flowering from early winter to early spring.

Appearance

A tall deciduous shrub bearing pointed-ovate, toothed leaves. The male catkins, which appear before the leaves, are distinctive and yellowish when mature; those of the female flowers, borne on the same tree, are very small and stalkless, but have bright red styles. The fruit is a nut or 'cob' encased in an unevenly jagged, green husk.

Traditions and associations

Hazel has become most widely known for providing the wood for divining or dowsing rods in the location of underground water sources and other objects. How the technique functions is unknown, but the fact that it works seems in little doubt. To make it effective the rod is traditionally cut from the tree on 23 June, the Eve of St John's Day. In the Austrian Tyrol, the rods must only be cut on Good Friday. Nowadays, however, dowsers tend to use artificial rods because of the difficulty in selecting forked Hazel wands that are properly balanced. Hazel divining rods have been employed throughout the British Isles not only to search out water but also, until the seventeenth century when such practices became too strongly linked with witchcraft, to pinpoint hidden treasure and the whereabouts of felons.

Hazel has also played an important part in Celtic lore in both fertility and fire rituals as well as possession of a protective magic. As the *Coll* it is one of the holy or Bile trees of Ireland for which the wanton felling was once a capital offence. In the Irish *Dinnshenchas* there lies a description of the nine Hazels of poetry, which overhang a sacred pool known as Connla's Well near Tipperary, and which allegedly produce both flowers and fruit simultaneously. The story goes that the salmon swimming in the well feed off the nuts, and the number of these they swallow is represented by the spots on their back. Hazelnuts have been regarded as fruits of wisdom, and the Salmon of Knowledge was a staple feature of Irish legend. Finn mac Cool, one of the earliest rulers of Ireland (literally the Son of Hazel) and a great hero of Irish folklore, is said to have acquired wisdom by sucking his thumb while visiting the poet Finneces who lived by the Boyne and guarded the salmon. He did so, the story goes, while one of the fish was cooking in the pot.

For children the Hazel has had no such connotations. In the last century they used the fruits for a game, perhaps the forerunner of marbles, called 'cobs', hence the popular name 'cob nuts'.

Holly *(Ilex aquifolium)*

Where and when

Holly is widespread and very common throughout Europe as far as the Caucasus, though thinning out markedly in colder northern regions where it is unable to survive severe winters. The plant grows in woods, scrubland, thickets and hedgerows, and the flowering season is from May to August. Fruiting occurs late in the year and typically coincides with Christmas.

Appearance

Generally growing as a shrub, but sometimes reaching the height of a small tree, Holly bears thick, glossy evergreen leaves on short stalks. These vary in that some are more or less entire while others are uneven and bordered with coarse, spiny teeth. The small, white male and female flowers, although similar in appearance, are borne in the leaf axils on different trees, and the fruit is a glossy, red berry.

Traditions and associations

Today the Holly is, of course, most strongly associated with the Christmas season as a symbol of life in winter but, according to Robert Graves, it may not have been the original tree to take the role. The accolade may have gone to the Evergreen Oak or Kerm Oak (*Quercus ilex*) which grew in Classical Greece and Rome and was originally introduced into the British Isles in the sixteenth century.

The Holly has always possessed strong significance in pagan Europe as a tree of the winter Solstice. In traditions of witchcraft, it is the Holly King who replaces the Oak King in the transition from summer and life, to winter and death. In Welsh mythology the two engage in battle each and every Mayday. In the traditional Anglicized tale of *Sir Gawain and the Green Knight*, which is an allegory of the battle of the seasons, Sir Gawain (who represents the Oak and summer) and The Green Knight (who represents Holly and winter) vow to behead each other at each midwinter and midsummer solstice.

According to the Roman writer, Pliny, the branches of Holly (probably *Quercus ilex*) defend houses from lightning and witchcraft, and this notion has also persisted throughout much of medieval Europe. Under Christian influence, Jesus Christ came to represent the Holly Lord, and the

word *holly* is a corruption of *holy*. Thus Holly is part of the traditional decoration of Christmas, and the old carol runs thus: 'Of all the trees that are in the wood, the Holly bears the crown.' Although it has been regarded as an essentially lucky tree, it is still considered a portent of ill luck to bring Holly into the house before Christmas Eve and it is essential to remove it before Twelfth Night. For some inexplicable reason, those sprigs put up in churches only have to be removed by Candlemas (2 February). To burn Holly on the fire has been to court disaster before the year is out, and to bring Holly in blossom into the house is generally thought to be unwise.

Holly has long been regarded as a useful medicinal tree and modern herbalists use the berries as a fever-suppressant. The leaves, when dried and mixed with tea, are employed as a tonic. A more rugged use was claimed in the Peak District of Derbyshire for the treatment of chilblains, which were supposed to disappear if the feet were thrashed with switches of Holly.

Lilac *(Syringa* spp.)

Where and when

Mainly native to eastern Europe and Asia, the Lilac is not indigenous to the British Isles but is extensively planted as an ornamental, and numerous cultivars have been developed from the 30 or so known species. These small and pretty flowering trees are members of the Olive family (Oleaceae), and flower in early and high summer.

Appearance

The Common Lilac (*Syringa vulgaris*) is a sturdy shrub or small tree which bears mid-green, pointed-ovate leaves. The lilac-coloured flowers are borne in erect, dense, triangular panicles which appear during May and June, and from this species are developed most of the popular hybrids, including the pure white *S. vulgaris* 'Vestale' shown here.

Traditions and associations

Tradition has it that the Lilac came to Europe from Persia and was extended to both the British Isles and the Americas by the Puritans. For many people it is a flower of ill luck, though there is controversy about whether this orginated because purple is a colour of mourning. Many white flowers are also linked with death, and white Lilac is no exception, for which reason it is considered unlucky to bring it into the house when in bloom. The blossoms normally possess four petals but, in conflict with the benefit of discovering a four-leaved clover, to find a Lilac flower with five petals is dangerous and represents the harbinger of disaster. One of the origins claimed in folklore for the white variety involves a true 'Mills and Boon' saga of an English nobleman and a trusting yet slighted girl. Having caused her death from a broken heart, the villain of the piece placed a mound of Lilac blossoms on her grave in the churchyard of a hamlet (unnamed) on the River Wye in Herefordshire. In the morning, to everyone's complete astonishment, the flowers had become white.

There is an equally old proverb that she who wears Lilac will never wear a wedding ring, and to send one's promised partner a sprig of Lilac was considered a delicate way of breaking off an engagement.

Aside from associations with love and death, the flowers of Lilac can foretell the weather. If they appear, but take a long time to open, it means fine weather, whereas if the flowers are late a rainy summer is promised.

Norway Spruce (*Picea abies*)

Where and when

Although not native to the British Isles, Norway Spruce has been extensively planted as a timber crop and is also cultivated as the most favoured 'Christmas Tree'.

Appearance

The Norway Spruce is a coniferous evergreen with an upright, conical shape and bearing numerous small, needlelike leaves. In common with other conifers, it bears male and female cones, the former (in which pollen and seeds develop) being short-lived.

Traditions and Associations

Although several kinds of conifer have been used in Christmas festivities, the Norway Spruce has been the most popular species since the nineteenth century when the tradition of decorating evergreen trees became widespread. The adornment of trees as the embodiment of the mother goddess has, however, been an integral part of New Year rites since pre-Christian times.

The concept of the 'Tree of Life' probably originated in the ancient Near East in New Year rites which were held in the spring. Among the earliest references to tree worship is one which involves the ill-fated Anatolian god, Attis. According to legend, he castrated himself beneath the sacred tree of the goddess Kybele and bled to death, whereupon his corpse became a Pine tree. The Romans honoured Attis on the Day of Blood, arguably the precedent of Easter, which included horrific rites of self-mutilation in emulation of the violent fate of the god. The rites were heralded by a Pine tree which was carried into the temple of Kybele, the honour being entrusted to a Guild of Tree Bearers who hung a model of Attis from its boughs, swathed it in woollen bands and decorated it with violets.

In pagan Scandinavia, Adam of Bremen describes a tree which dominated a sacred grove beside the temple in the old Swedish spiritual centre of Uppsala: 'beside this temple stands an enormous tree, spreading its branches far and wide; it is evergreen in winter and summer. No one knows what kind of tree it is . . .' This, too, was the recipient of bloody sacrifice of human and animal victims.

Direct links between such pagan roots and modern Christmas traditions are unproven although it has to be accepted that the early Christian Church borrowed extensively from pagan Roman culture. The midwinter solstice, which was regarded as the Nativity of the Sun in the dominant cult of Mithras, fell, according to the Julian calendar, on 25 December, and the Christian Church chose to adopt the date for the celebration of the birth of Jesus. Thus many of the Mithraic customs, which themselves owed heavily to ancient Near Eastern traditions and which involved reverence to sacred trees, were adopted by the fledgling Christian community.

Legend has it that the eighth-century missionary, St Boniface, cut down a sacred Oak in Germany on Christmas Eve and as it fell a Fir sapling emerged. Boniface was inspired to adopt the Fir as an emblem of Christian faith. Other mythology suggests that as Martin Luther was walking home under a starry sky he was moved to dig up a Fir tree as a frame for candles to remind his children of the stars in the Christian heaven. In England, Charlotte, the wife of George III, had a Christmas tree erected at Windsor, while in Victorian times Albert, the Prince Consort, initiated the seasonal import of Firs from his native Coburg. The ancient pagan tradition of decorating holy trees with rags and strips of cloth has, almost certainly, been modernized into the Victorian ceremony of dressing the Christmas tree with gifts, lights and baubles.

Oaks (*Quercus* spp.)

Where and when

A member of probably the best-known family of trees throughout Europe (Fagaceae), the native British Oak (*Quercus robur*) extends throughout the Continent and into parts of central Asia, although it tends to be replaced by the evergreen species of Ilex Oak (*Q. ilex*) in southern Europe, the Turkey Oak (*Q. cerris*) in southeastern Europe and the Cork Tree (*Q. suber*) in the south-western parts of the Continent. The American Red Oak (*Q. rubra*) has also become naturalized in many areas. The Oaks possess great longevity, belong to the same group of trees as the Beeches, and are common in woods and hedgerows, although they prefer richer soils.

Appearance

The tree develops with a characteristic broad crown supported by a massive, often gnarled, trunk with a rough, grey-brown bark. The flowers take the form of separate male catkins and solitary, inconspicuous, female flowers which mature to produce acorn fruits in scaly cups. The leaves are oblong and lobed, on short stalks, those of the Turkey Oak being noticeably more jagged.

Traditions and associations

A handsome and resolute tree, great mystery and magic has always surrounded the Oak, and it is not surprising that British forces and their vessels have, in the past, been dubbed 'Hearts of Oak'. Its mystical associations extend back at least to the Celtic era and probably to prehistoric times. To the Greeks it was the tree sacred to Zeus, and one of the most famous of all oracular sanctuaries is that of the Oak at Dodona. In the *Iliad* of Homer, Odysseus travels to Dodona to learn 'the plans of Zeus from the oak of lofty foliage' and in Hesiod's *Catalogues* he describes how priestesses, 'the doves', live in the hollow of its trunk and 'from them the men of earth carry away all kinds of prophecy – whosoever fares to that spot and questions the deathless god, and comes bringing gifts with good omens'. On Mount Lyceus, the link between Zeus as god of the Oaks and of storms was made in a rite during which the priest dipped an Oak bough into the water of a sacred spring. The Romans predictably followed the Greek vogue by dedicating the Oak to Jupiter, but they also dedicated it to the old Italic fire goddess, Vesta, for whom a sacred fire of Oak logs, tended by the virginal *vestales*, burned eternally in a small temple at the foot of the Palatine Hill. At Roman weddings, Oak boughs were carried, for reasons which are not entirely clear, as symbols of fertility.

There is, however, some statistical evidence to indicate that the Oak attracts lightning strikes more than any other tree, and this may provide one explanation of why it became associated with thunder gods.

For the Celts, across Europe, the Oak was a sacred tree and the groves in which their priesthood, the Druids, performed bloody rituals were universally feared by the Roman empire-builders. The Roman author Lucan, writing in the first century BC about a Celtic sanctuary near Marseilles that was destroyed during Caesar's campaigns, summed up the mood:

> *A grove there was, untouched by men's hands from ancient times whose interlacing boughs enclosed a space of darkness and cold shade, and banished the sunlight from above. No rural Pan dwelt there, nor Silvanus, ruler of the woods, no nymphs; but gods were worshipped there with savage rites, the altars were heaped with hideous offerings, and every tree was sprinkled with human gore. On these boughs, if antiquity, reverential of the gods, deserves any credit, birds feared to perch; in those coverts wild beasts would not lie down; no wind ever bore down upon that wood, nor thunderbolt*

hurled from black clouds; the trees, even when they spread their leaves to no breeze, rustled among themselves. Water also fell there in abundance from dark springs. The images of the gods, grim and rude, were uncouth blocks formed of felled tree trunks.

Arguably, the Greek word for the Oak (*druz*) is the derivation of the term Druid. There is a similar Gaelic word *derwydd* which means 'oak-seer'. It is interesting to note that, in much of the old literature, the Mistletoe, a plant which was also sacred to the Druids, is said to grow on Oak, though modern experience suggests that it is more common on other trees.

The Germanic and Norse cultures copied the Classical theme in as much as they dedicated the Oak to their thunder gods, respectively Donar and Thor, and this theme, linking the tree with storm gods, appears to have been largely emulated throughout the Aryan regions. It suggests that the Oak was peculiarly revered as a holy tree by the prehistoric Aryan stock who lived in a world dominated by the vast Hercynian forests which extended unbroken across enormous reaches of the Continent.

The Oak has long been associated with the fertility of summer and, arguably, the Irish hero, Cu Chulain, represents the Oak King. In English legend he becomes Sir Gawain and does annual battle with the Green Knight, who is armed with a massive Holly club and represents winter.

One of the traditions of Medieval witchcraft has been to burn an Oak log in a hearth on Midsummer's Eve. This fire is then tended until the same date the following year, when the embers are removed to make way for a new log and the ashes, mixed with seed corn, are scattered on the earth. The rite largely echoes the ceremony of burning the Yule log which was also traditionally cut from Oak.

There is also some suggestion that, in ancient times, the kindling of the Oak fire was accompanied by a human sacrifice representing the Oak Spirit or the Oak King. The priest of the Oak grove at Nemi was almost certainly slaughtered as a fertility offering to the goddess Diana. According to Frazer (in *The Golden Bough*), the slaughter of the Norse god Balder with a shaft of Mistletoe indicates that he was the apotheosis of the Oak, although this particular theory appears somewhat tenuous. It is also well recorded that from the early Bronze Age in Scandinavia coffins were hollowed out from Oak trunks. The body was laid inside on cow hide and surrounded by flowers, and the two halves of the trunk were tightly sealed before burial.

Frazer also describes a quaint Shropshire custom which was based on the belief that the Oak blooms on Midsummer's Eve and the flowers wither before daybreak. In order to ascertain the identity of her future husband, a maiden should spread a small sheet beneath the Oak and catch the remains of the blossoms. These, when placed under her pillow, will cause her to dream of her future bridegroom.

More recently the various Druid clans still worship regularly in the presence of these trees. In the 1950s, a Californian group, the Live Oak Grove, went so far as to plant a sacred grove.

The witch-writer, Doreen Valiente, quotes a popular old rhyme from the New Forest in Hampshire, based on the belief that to turn one's cloak inside out and to wear it thus was a protection against being distracted from your path by fairies who reside in Oak trees: 'Turn your cloaks, for fairy folks are in old oaks.' She also describes an old piece of lore from Sussex that to carry an acorn about one's person is an assurance of youthful health and vitality. The association of the Oak with luck may also account, to some extent, for the frequent use of acorns and Oak sprigs in old wood-carvings, particularly on doors, newel and gateposts. The Oak in spring has been thought to indicate the coming season's weather with the rhyme: 'If the Oak before the Ash, we shall only get a splash. If the Ash before the Oak, we shall surely get a soak; '

Rowan *(Sorbus aucuparia)*

Where and when

Also commonly known as the Mountain Ash, Rowan is found in woodlands throughout Europe and parts of northwest Asia growing, as its name suggests, particularly in mountainous and hilly districts where it tolerates dryness and rocky soils, although in such locations it may become shrublike. It also planted as an ornamental in many lowland places from where it has escaped and become naturalized. In Britain, it is particularly common in the north and west. It flowers in high summer.

Appearance

Growing, other than at higher altitudes, as a moderately sized tree with a smooth, grey bark, Rowan bears regularly pinnate leaves with 11–19 pairs of toothed, lance-shaped leaflets. The flowers, which appear in May and June, are white, small and numerous, arranged in corymbs at the end of short branches. These mature into small bright red or orange-red berries which hang in clusters.

Traditions and associations

The Rowan has been much associated with witchcraft both as a tool of witches and, conversely, as a defence against them. In upland localities it has taken on some of the mystique that the Hawthorn enjoys in lowland areas, and in Iceland there is a tradition that hints at the *Cad Goddeu* ('Battle of the Trees') found in Welsh mythology. It is said that the Rowan and the Juniper are sworn enemies and that any tree planted between the two adversaries will be split in two by their warring.

The Rowan berry was considered by the Classical philosophers to be one of the sacred foods of the gods, and the Celtic Druids believed that it possessed great magical and divinatory properties. Its oracular function was respected throughout many parts of pagan Europe. According to John Lightfoot's *Flora Scotica* of 1777, the presence of Rowan trees in the vicinity of upland stone circles is too frequent to be coincidental. The magical wand made from Rowan wood was known as the Witch Wand, and is still regarded by many witches as an indispensable tool.

In company with such herbs as Dill and Vervain, Rowan has been regarded as a guard against witches and the injuries that they can reputedly inflict in various ways. Rowan trees were planted close to houses as a form of protection, superstitious country people often carried a piece of Rowan in their pocket, and the doorway or the chimneybreast of a house or barn might be hung with Rowan twigs as a safeguard against evil. Particularly at Beltane, on the eve of Mayday, it was thought that witches were out and about in force stealing cow's milk and creating all sorts of mayhem, so, to counter the consequences of these excursions, Rowan branches were placed across the doors of cowsheds. Rowan crosses tied to cows' tails and Rowan carter's whips were both useful devices to protect animals against witchcraft. By the same token, domestic animals that were known to be bewitched could only be controlled through the application of a Rowan stick. The wood has also been considered a particularly effective magical protection against lightning strikes and the tree, in common with some others including Hawthorn, has provided a country weather vane. An abundance of fruit has been taken as a warning of a poor crop in the cornfields with little to do at harvest time:'Many rains, many Rowans, Many Rowans, many yawns.'

It should also be mentioned that Rowan berries have been linked with poisoning cases in children who, attracted by their bright colour, have consumed them. Unfortunately, although it is a member of the Rose family, the Rowan's fruits do contain toxins.

Willows (*Salix* spp.)

Where and when

Because they generally favour damp ground with a high water table, Willows are typically seen growing along the banks of rivers and streams and in bogs and marshes. At least 15 species are indigenous in the British Isles and include among their commoner members the Bay, Crack and Common Willows, the Osier and the Sallow. The Weeping Willow (*Salix babylonica*), which is an Asiatic introduction widely cultivated in Europe for its decorative value, is a common sight away from water in parks and gardens. Willows hybridize very readily and almost 50 varieties are currently recognized.

Appearance

The Willows are all deciduous and range from creeping shrubs to tall trees, many with a somewhat palmlike character to their boughs. Most bear slim, alternate leaves and all develop small flowers in catkins on separate trees, the male inflorescence being the more obvious.

The Crack Willow (*S. fragilis*), that which is most commonly seen pollarded on river banks, grows into a tall tree with widely angled branches, while the Common or White Willow (*S. alba*) has a more upright habit. The Osiers are shrubs which rarely grow beyond 5 metres (15 ft) and the Common Sallow (*S. caprea*) is the source of 'palms' at Easter and its near relative the Pussy or Bay Willow (*S. pentandra*) bears the earliest of the large seasonal catkins.

Traditions and associations

There are hints in the oldest cuneiform texts dating back to the third millennium BC that Willow may have been one of the first trees in the ancient Near East to possess religious significance as the embodiment of the goddess of life. She was known as Inana to the Sumerians and became the Ishtar of the Akkadians and Babylonians. Such a tree may have grown on the banks of the Euphrates and, in the texts, was called the *hulub* or *haluppu*. By the time of the Akkadian dynasty, this tree had become depicted as a heavily stylized and abstracted totem, the religious significance of which was evident until as late as 200 BC. In Syrio-Palestine this totem was described as the *asherah* and, as a rallying point for disenchanted Israelites, it was a major thorn in the flesh of the orthodox priests. Described euphemistically as the 'grove' in the King James version of the Old Testament, the *asherah* was installed in the Temple of Jerusalem by those rulers of Israel who elected to backslide into observation of the alien fertility religions practised in states which encompassed them.

To the Greeks and Romans, the Willow was the tree of Hecate, the feared goddess of magic, the moon and nocturnal journeys, of Selene, the other moon goddess who fused with Hecate in the Hellenistic period and of Persephone, the ill-fated queen of the Underworld. Perhaps, in part, because of these associations, Willow also became closely linked with the Druids and with witchcraft. The terrible 'wicker man' in which human and animal sacrifices were burnt alive and which was the subject of a 1960s cult classic film starring Edward Woodward, was described fleetingly and at second hand by Julius Caesar in his *Gallic Wars*, and was allegedly constructed from the supple wands of Osier.

The witch's besom broom is traditionally constructed of Birch twigs bound to an Ash shaft with Osier strips. In apparent conflict, the leaves and bark were once employed as an effective remedy against the aches and pains inflicted on their victims by malevolent witches, because the tissues of Willow synthesize salicylic acid, the basic ingredient of aspirin.

As the tree of Selene, the Willow was strongly associated with the moon, whose tears generate the morning dew, and under the aegis of western Christianity it became a symbol of grief, strongly associated with Passiontide and Easter. Many churches were, and still are, decorated with sprays of Willow on Palm Sunday. Willow also reflected grief at a more personal level, as was indicated by Swan in the *Speculum Mundi* of 1635: 'It is yet a custom that he which is deprived of his love must wear a willow garland.' One of the most famous poems of grief, the 'Willow Song' from Act IV of Shakespeare's *Othello*, which was further popularized in Verdi's opera, relates:

My mother had a maid called Barbara
She was in love and he she loved proved mad
And did forsake her. She had a song of willow;
An old thing 'twas, but it expressed her fortune,
And she died singing it.

As with so many plants associated with magic and mystery, Willow has been linked with beliefs of contradictory nature. On the one hand, it has been considered unlucky to bring Willow into the house in spring in some parts of England, while in other local areas a gift of Willow on Mayday morning was regarded as a boon.

Yew *(Taxus baccata)*

Where and when

Spread throughout Europe, northern Asia and North America, it is common in Britain, where it was planted extensively in earlier times and is indigenous in hilly regions. Individual trees can attain great age.

Appearance

An evergreen spreading tree or shrub with dark, needlelike leaves, arranged pinnately. The stout trunks consist of extremely hard wood and are clothed with a scaly, reddish-brown bark. Male and female flowers appear on separate trees, the small male catkins emerging first and characterized by large numbers of yellow stamens. The female inflorescence is greenish and egg-shaped and matures into a coral-pink, fleshy fruit surrounding the single seed.

Traditions and associations

To the ancient world, the Yew was the tree of death and the association has never been wholly been lost, as anyone visiting a churchyard today will understand. In the Classical eras of Greece and Rome, the Yew was sacred to Hecate, the chthonic goddess who controls the pathways of the night, complete with howling dogs and a ghostly retinue. The Romans made sacrifices to Hecate of black bulls, and on the necks of these they placed wreaths of Yew. It was the soldiers of Greece and Rome who first used bows made from Yew wood and who probably also discovered the deadly efficacy of taxine, the alkaloid produced by the tree, when rubbed into the tips of their arrows. The Celts either learned of the poison independently or from the Romans, since they also applied a cocktail of juices, including that of Yew, to their weapons. It is the infamous 'hebanon' which the uncle of Hamlet used to poison the king in Shakespeare's play, and in *Macbeth* it is one of the ingredients in the Witches' cauldron. All parts except for the ripe flesh around the seed are intensely poisonous.

Yew wood is extraordinarily hard and resistant to decay and for this reason it has been preferred for making bows and arrows as well as fine furniture. The Irish also used it to fashion the staves of wine barrels, for which reason the timber was known as 'the coffin of the vine'.

Yew has been closely associated with the rites of passage between life and death. In the Irish legend of Deirdriu, the daughter of the chieftain Felim Mac Dall, and Naoise, the son of Usna, the pair fall in love and flee the wrath of Cochobhar, the king, to whom Deirdriu is officially betrothed. They are persuaded to return to Ireland but the invitation is a trap, Naoise is slain and Deirdriu becomes the unwilling bride of Cochobhar until she chooses suicide. According to one version of the tale Cochobhar attempts to keep the two apart in death by driving Yew stakes through their bodies, but the design fails because the stakes sprout and become trees which eventually entwine their branches above the cathedral of Armagh. In other traditions, in England, the Yew standing beside the graveyard path is believed to oversee the separation of the spirit from the body.

P A R T   T H R E E

Fungi

PART THREE

Fungi

Introduction

WE HAVE NEVER quite been able to come to terms with the extraordinary life-forms which are more commonly referred to as mushrooms and toadstools, and it is our constant puzzlement about their nature which has done much, over the centuries, to fuel our view of them as objects of mystery and magic.

Arguably the greatest of all classifiers and sorters of living things, the eighteenth-century Swedish botanist, Carl Linnaeus, gave up on them, having successfully introduced the binomial system of naming and positioning in respect of the rest of the natural world. His dismissive observation of the fungi put them down as 'thieving and various beggars which seize upon the odds and ends which plants leave behind them when Flora is leading them into winter quarters'. It was left to Linnaeus' successor and compatriot, Elias Fries, to group fungi into some semblance of order, based not on their external morphology (which was already known to be an impossibility), but on the colour of their microscopic spores. In some respects, our ambivalence towards fungi has changed little. In recent years it has been concluded that they fit conveniently into neither the animal nor the plant kingdoms and that the only sensible recourse is to provide them with their own quite separate department of biology.

Our attitude is not entirely surprising, since the fungi are like nothing else that exists in nature. They appear, at first glance, to be plants, yet they possess shapes, textures and colours that are peculiar to themselves. They do not feed like other plants, they possess no chlorophyll, they appear to generate no seeds, they emerge with astonishing speed when the rest of the green world is dying and, as Pliny once put it succinctly: 'How is it that anything can spring up and live without a root?' When one considers that they live in dank and gloomy woodlands, already the province of much that is sacred and esoteric, that they offer luminosity, hallucinogens and poisons and accompany these sinister attributes with generating fairy rings, and growing up with phallic and other weird appearances such as ears, blackened fingers, testicles and brains, it is not surprising that the fungi provide a field in which the human imagination can happily run riot.

For the tribal priest or shaman living in a simple, nomadic culture, the powers of certain fungi unlock the door to the heavens. They possess a latent energy which, in a primitive context, is as enormous as the power of the atomic bomb or the most powerful microchip. Ownership of the magic of the hallucinogenic and the deadly can place men of intelligence and vision infinitely higher than their peers, a strength which has dictated that such material should be used only by the right people and at the proper time, accompanied by the correct ritual and with the knowledge that a legend has to be created to account for not only the usage but also the beginnings. Ownership and use of certain mushrooms has, thus, been regulated through strict taboos.

To these earliest sentiments must be added further layers of a logic that was deprived of scientific and technological understanding. It was recognized in the Classical world that certain types of fungi were lethally poisonous – the wife of the Emperor Claudius achieved singular notoriety for her part in dispatching the ruler of the Roman Empire when she laced his evening meal with the juices of the Death Cap (*Amanita phalloides*) – and it was wrongly assumed that their toxicity was absorbed by the tissues of the mushrooms from other objects. Writing in the second century AD, the Sicilian physician and herbalist Dioscorides made the following typical observation: 'Fungi have a twofold difference, for they are either good for food or poisonous; their poisonous nature

The risqué shape of the Stinkhorn embarrassed the prudish Victorians.

depends on various causes, for either such fungi grow amongst rusty nails or rotten rags, or near serpents' holes, or on trees producing noxious fruits; such have a thick coating of mucus, and when laid by after being gathered, quickly become putrid.'

One of the very earliest recorded observations, that of the Greek Nicander, includes the observation: 'Let not the evil ferment of the earth which often causes swellings in the belly or strictures in the throat, distress a man; for when it has grown up under the viper's hollow track it gives forth the poison and hard breathing of its mouth; men generally call the ferment by the name of fungus.'

These myths and fallacies were faithfully supported, more or less, until the Age of Enlightenment came and the eighteenth-century botanists adopted a less fanciful approach. In the interim, remarkably little progress had been made in understanding fungi or their effects on the human body, an unfortunate shortcoming since among the ranks of mushroom species are members which synthesize some of the most virulent toxins known to man. Even after the dawn of scientific understanding, the 'old wives' tales' persisted, and these were often focused with particular regard to poisonous fungi. Those that were dangerous to eat reputedly blackened silver spoons, would not peel, were avoided by animals, possessed bright colours and their cut flesh changed colour. Much of this misinformation stemmed from notions that properly belonged in the Dark Ages, and resulted in many fatalities. Even today, some of the spurious lore has not been entirely eradicated from the mushroom-hunting culture.

Literature has done much to swell our sentiment about fungi as unwholesome growths associated with death and decay. In *The Fall of the House of Usher*, Edgar Allen Poe uses such notions to chilling effect. 'Fungi overspread the whole exterior, hanging in a fine tangled web from the eaves. There was much in this that reminded me of the specious totality of old woodwork which has rotted long years in some neglected vault with no disturbance from the breath of the external air.' While Poe's account resides in the realms of fiction rather than biological accuracy, it is undeniable that the smell, positioning and appearance of the Dry Rot Fungus (*Serpula lacrimans*) offers the most sinister connotations. In Biblical times the presence of this species in a house was described in terms of a divine visitation of plague:

> *The priest shall command that they empty the house, before the priest go into it to see the plague, that all that is in the house be not made unclean: and afterwards the priest shall go in to see the house; and he shall look on the plague, and, behold, if the plague be in the walls of the house with hollow strakes, greenish or reddish, which in sight are lower than the wall; then the priest shall go out of the house to the door of the house, and shut up the house seven days . . .*
>
> (Leviticus 14, 36 and 37)

In the cult sci-fi classic of the early years of television, *The Quatermass Experiment*, the victim returned from deep space infected with some alien germ that manifested itself by turning him into something that looked, for a while, distinctly fungoid, and this has been echoed in numerous copycat scenarios.

A sentient part of us, aided and abetted by folklore and fiction, still sees fungi in terms of witches, hobgoblins and fairies. An oddly distorted species of Jelly Fungus, *Exidia glandulosa*, an unpleasantly black and greasy-looking specimen that infests the rotting branches of deciduous trees, is still commonly referred to as Witches' Butter, sustaining the age-old myth that it is a by-product of the clandestine milking of cows by aged and toothless crones wearing pointy hats and riding on broomsticks in the dead of night.

Devil's Bolete (*Boletus satanas*)

Where and when

Also known as Satan's Bolete, this striking fungus appears rarely but prefers chalk or limestone soils under Oak and Beech, and it fruits from late summer to early autumn.

Appearance

A massive structure possessing a chalk-white or very pale cream, bun-shaped cap, extending up to 25 cm (10 in) in diameter, with reddish-orange pores beneath, supported by an equally robust, bulbous, reddish-netted stem which can be as much as 10 cm (4 in) in diameter, and which is more yellowish towards the apex. There is no ring on the stem. The tubes leading to the pores are at first yellowish becoming tinged olive with age, and the flesh throughout turns blue, slowly, when cut or damaged.

Traditions and associations

The Devil's Bolete is dangerously poisonous to human beings, though innocuous to an assortment of other animals, which results in the flesh often being slug-eaten. This toadstool has, predictably, acquired all kinds of sinister tags, and traditionally it is presumed to be left behind when the Devil passes by in the dark hours of the night. It has also been linked with the Witch's Sabbat and the passage of the infamous Wild Hunt described in the English ninth-century *Bishop's Canon*. The enormous dimensions of the fruiting body and the startling white and red colours have assisted with its reputation and, even to a seasoned fungus-hunter, it presents a provocative sight rising from a gloomy woodland floor. White is a colour traditionally associated with death, and red has always been a colour representing danger or evil. The effect of poisoning is severe gastro-enteritis, which may persist for many hours and has been known to result in death.

Ergot *(Claviceps purpurea)*

Where and when

Much less common than in previous centuries, as a consequence of the screening of grain and the application of fungicides to crops, the fruiting bodies, or sclerotia, are still occasionally to be found infecting the ears of Rye Grasses and, less frequently still, other grass species. The sclerotia appear from summer to autumn, while the much smaller and less obvious perithecial stage over-winters on the ground.

Appearance

The sclerotium is small, only 5–10 mm (¼ – ½ in) in length, and is black, somewhat curved and spindle-shaped, and it develops in the inflorescence of the host plant. If a sclerotium is split open, it reveals white flesh inside.

Traditions and associations

In medical terms, *Claviceps purpurea* causes the disease known as ergotism. Although it has largely been eradicated, it occasionally reappears in impoverished or backward rural communities. The last major outbreak in the British Isles occurred among Jewish immigrants in Manchester in 1927, while in the same year more than 11,000 cases were reported in an epidemic that swept parts of Russia. As recently as 1977, though, about 136 cases were reported from the Wollo region of Ethiopia.

The fungus synthesizes toxins which, although complex, are all based on lysergic acid which has a pronounced effect on the smooth, involuntary muscle of the body, causing it to contract. For this reason, ergot was popular as a back-street abortifacient, and with midwives in times gone by as an aid to speeding up delivery. The side-effects are, however, severe, and the practice has been discontinued.

Serious problems occur when ergot is ingested over a period of time through consumption of Rye bread made from infected flour. This leads to chronic ergotism, which takes two distinct forms. The first, convulsive ergotism, was mainly observed in Russia and her neighbours, the first recorded outbreak occurring in 1722. The symptoms begin with swelling of the limbs and the sense of extremes of heat and cold. This is accompanied by great pain and the sensation of 'ants running about under the skin'. After a week or so these initial symptoms lead to muscle spasm, convulsions and paralysis. A ravenous appetite can also manifest itself, with deranged victims eating vast amounts of food and even clothing and faeces. The other form, gangrenous ergotism, was experienced most widely in France with similar initial symptoms, after which the affected areas become numb, and the skin blue and cold or cyanosed. This marks the onset of dry gangrene, when the limb turns black, and the only remedy has been amputation. Alternatively, without treatment, it has not been unknown for an arm or leg to fall off of its own accord.

Although first recorded at the beginning of the eleventh century, until comparatively recently the cause of this dreadful disease was entirely unknown, and the Church was quick to attribute to it the label of some form of divine retribution. It became known in France as *Le Feu de St Antoine* (St Anthony's Fire), a condition graphically described in old fifteenth- and sixteenth-century woodcuts in which the victim is depicted, begging to St Anthony for relief, accompanied by flames and adopting a staggering gait, the limbs and fingers flexed like claws and the mouth open in a rictus of agony. It was not until 1771 that the French Abbé Teissier established a positive scientific link between *Claviceps* sclerotia and the disease. In experiments, feeding infected Rye grain to ducks and pigs, he discovered that they developed characteristic symptoms.

St Anthony of Padua lived as a recluse in remote tombs in the Egyptian desert during the

fourth century AD and was, by tradition, the second Christian hermit (following in the footsteps of his mentor St Paul of Thebes), although his fame is probably attributable more to the fact that a glowing and much translated biography was compiled by a contemporary, Athanasius, the Patriarch of Alexandria, and St Anthony became a role model for pious Catholics throughout Europe. His emblems include a book, a bell, a swine, and flames, and he was believed to possess a holy power over fire and flame; thus the disease of ergotism was also known as the *Ignis Sacer* (Sacred Fire). Among its alternative names was *Ignis Beatae Virginis* (Fire of the Blessed Virgin). The fear of causing St Anthony's displeasure by blasphemy and other means, and of his causing death 'by inner burning' in response, was very real in the minds of Medieval communities. Conversely, it was believed that he could relieve sufferers of the condition. Early in the sixteenth century, William Tyndale wrote, 'Who dare deny St Anthony a fleece of wool for fear of his terrible fire, or lest he send the pox among our sheep?' The relics of the saint were eventually interred at the church of La Motte au Bois in Vienne, and pilgrimages of the sick became so popular that eventually a hospital was built nearby, its walls decorated, appropriately, with red flames.

There are also suggestions that cases which were recorded as diabolical possession of women, particularly those which occurred in French nunneries, may have been more properly attributable to chronic ergot poisoning.

Fairy Ring Mushroom

(Marasmius oreades)

Where and when

Rings appear on soil amid short grass in pastures and lawns throughout a large part of the year, from spring to autumn, and are a common sight until the first frosts. The fruiting bodies are also capable of withstanding considerable periods of drought, shrivelling in dry conditions but quickly reviving when the weather becomes damp.

Appearance

A small but fleshy mushroom, pale tan in colour when damp, but drying to cream or buff, with a blunt boss in the centre of the cap and a tough stem. The cap measures 2–5 cm (¾–2 in) in diameter and the gills are whitish, becoming cream,

free from the top of the stalk and somewhat distant from one another. The stem has a resistant, almost cartilaginous texture, there is no ring, and it is generally rooting. The taste of the flesh is slightly peppery, although care must be taken not to confuse this mushroom with the dangerously poisonous *Clitocybe dealbata* and *C. rivulosa*, both of which are of similar size and habit.

Traditions and Associations

These little mushrooms appear in almost perfect circles, a characteristic behaviour which led to all sorts of quaint tales and beliefs about the 'fairy ring'. In reality there is scant mystery, the ring patterns that sometimes extend for many metres across being attributable to the very regular growth of the underground vegetative mycelium from a central point and the habit of generating fruiting bodies only at the periphery. The grass immediately to the inside of the current year's fruiting bodies tends to be more luxuriant and darker than that of the surrounding turf because of nutrients generated in the soil by the fungus. These fairy rings can also survive for decades, perhaps even centuries, slowly increasing in diameter with each passing season.

The early herbalists had no idea of the scientific explanation for rings and they were clearly viewed as places of magic. Consequently the stories which have grown up surrounding the fairy rings are numerous and often not a little bizarre. The mushrooms were generally believed to grow on sites frequented by fairies or witches and to have been left behind after unspeakable goings-on at such times as Mayday Eve and Hallowe'en. Shakespeare's *The Tempest* includes this comment by Prospero, observing the 'little people': 'You demi-puppets that, by moonshine do the green sour ringlets make, whereof ewe not bites; and you, whose pastime is to make midnight mushrumps . . . '.

Elsewhere in Europe, variations on the theme have produced legends of mythical beasts perambulating and breathing or spitting on the grass. The turf immediately within the lush area can appear withered because of overstimulation, and this has prompted the notion of dragons scorching it with their fiery nostrils!

Because of the sacred connotation of the circle and the association with the supernatural, the idea of stepping inside the ring has been viewed with mixed emotions. It has been believed that if, on a May morning, a young girl bathes her face in the dew, her beauty will increase. If, however, she has the temerity to step, accidentally, within a fairy ring while performing her toilet, the fairies will take rapid offence at the intrusion and cause her skin to erupt in blotches and pimples. Conversely, many country folk have believed it lucky to have a fairy ring growing in their garden.

Neither has the scientific community of past ages been slow to come up with remarkable theories. Biological explanations have included moles conducting their mining operations in perfect circles, and cattle standing around munching on their communal piles of hay while their rear ends, in fanwise arrangement, fertilize neat rings in the grass. The most ludicrous theory of all was probably that invented by an early eighteenth-century observer named Bradley, whose opinion it was that the sex lives of slugs and snails lay at the core of the mystery. They promenaded, he claimed, in circles on his lawn, leaving, with each amorous turn, a trail of slime which putrefied and then turned into mushrooms.

Physicists put the occurrence of fairy rings down to nothing more prosaic than lightning strikes. It was not until 1792 that the correct scientific explanation was proposed.

Aside from its magical and mysterious connotations, Fairy Ring Mushroom or Champignon is an excellent edible species, and in days gone by country housewives would string the little caps on threads and dry them across the kitchen rafters before employing them in such recipes as steak and kidney pie.

Fly Agaric (*Amanita muscaria*)

Where and when

This distinctive fungus is to be found on poor or sandy soils, preferring association with Birches and Pines. The fruiting bodies appear, solitary or in scattered groups, during the late summer and autumn, continuing until the first frosts.

Appearance

The fruiting body has a typical mushroom shape and is large and fleshy, possessing all the obvious characteristics of the *Amanita* group. The domed cap, extending to 9–10 cm (3½–4 in) in diameter, is bright red with white patches which may become washed off by rain. As the fungus ages, the colour of the cap also sometimes fades to an orange-red. The patches are the remnants of the veil or volva that protected the young specimen as it pushed up through the soil. The gills beneath the cap are white, crowded and free; in other words they are not attached directly to the top of the stalk. The stalk is also white, extends up to 18 cm (7 in) tall and 2 cm (¾ in) wide and is solidly fleshy, smooth or slightly sculptured, apart from several warty rings immediately above

the bulbous base. Towards the top of the stem is a white, membranous, hanging ring with a double margin, the remnant of a secondary or partial veil.

Traditions and associations

This is the toadstool without which few fairy stories would be complete, and it is, of course, an indispensable aspect of the life and accommodation of Enid Blyton's famous characters, Noddy and Big Ears, partly on account of its strikingly attractive colours but also, no doubt, because of magical associations, which probably extend back to prehistoric times. Allegedly, though there is no substantiating evidence, the Druids used hallucinogenic mushrooms in their secret rituals and it was their probable ban on consumption by the rank and file, a taboo which was also mirrored by the Romans, that may have led to the present-day repugnance among many people in Britain.

Amanita muscaria also features in esoteric art, extending back to as early as the thirteenth century. Among the ruins of a church at Plaincourault in France, a fresco depicts a pregnant Eve standing beside the serpent which is entwined around a splendid representation of the mushroom. There is also some argument put forward by a number of authors that the mysterious Soma plant which constitutes the subject-matter of the ninth book of the *Rig Veda* in Hinduism is Fly Agaric or a similar species. In one poem the writer not only indicates that the plant grows in the mountainous region of Saryanavat but also invites the god Indra to drink the juice of Soma with him, and then asks the Soma to make him immortal as he becomes influenced by its hallucinogenic properties.

The deadly toxins found in the Death Cap (*A. phalloides*) are absent from Fly Agaric, but the fungus synthesizes two important chemical compounds, mycoatropine, a substance similar to choline, and small amounts of muscarinem, both of which have a pronounced effect on the human physiology.

The effects of poisoning are serious if the mushroom is consumed as part of a meal without proper preparation and by someone unused to its effects, the symptoms beginning after about three hours and including vomiting, diarrhoea, rapid breathing, slowed pulse and delirium. A number of nomadic tribes living in northern Europe until the turn of the century are known to have employed *A. muscaria* as a plant of great mystical and religious significance, in part for the esoteric reasons given at the beginning of this section but largely on account of its hallucinogenic properties. In order to make the material less noxious, it was first dried in the sun. Even so, the effect of the principal drug, mycoatropine, on the central nervous system was dramatic, causing giddiness and nervous excitation followed by a state of trance heightened by vivid hallucination.

During the first years of the twentieth century, the Swedish-American ethnologist, Waldemar Jochelson, spent considerable periods of time living among, and studying the customs of, primitive tribes in the remote and extremely harsh environment of the Kamchatka Peninsula in southeastern Siberia. These peoples were little removed from a Stone-Age style of life, and were shortly to be engulfed by the spread of Russian orthodoxy. They included a tribe called the Koryak, whose maritime bands chased seals and white whales in flimsy sealskin boats, while others hunted reindeer amid the sparse Pine and Birch woods running down from the mountains close to the sea. One of the shamankas (female shamans) told Jochelson an intriguing legend which exemplifies the mystical powers of the Fly Agaric:

> *Big Raven caught a whale, but he could not send it to its home in the sea. He was unable to lift the grass bag containing travelling provisions for the whale. Big Raven called to Existence to help. Existence said, 'Go to a level place near the sea; there you will find soft white*

stalks with red and white spotted hats. These are spirits, the Wapag. Eat some and they will help you.' Big Raven went to the place that Existence had told him of and meanwhile Existence spat on the Earth. Out of his saliva at the place where it fell, fungus appeared which Big Raven found and ate, and began to feel gay. He started to dance and the Wapag spirits of the fungus said to him, 'How is it that, though being such a strong man, you cannot lift the bag?' 'That is right,' said Big Raven. 'I am a strong man. I shall go and lift the travelling bag.' He went and lifted the bag and sent the whale home. The Wapag showed him the whale going out to sea and how it returned to its brothers and sisters. Big Raven said, 'Let the fungus remain on earth and let my children see what it will show them.'

(After Jochelson)

Big Raven, the hero of the story, is the first, mythical, all-powerful shaman of the Koryak tribe and much of his behaviour in various tales was emulated by the shamans that Jochelson met in 1900. Thus they too ate the sacred fungus of the Wapag spirits, though with a ritual which, at times, verged on the bizarre. It had been discovered by the Koryak and other neighbouring tribes that the narcotic was passed rapidly out of the body in the urine. The Fly Agaric was, at times, in limited supply and Jochelson found one group of shamans making judicious use of the available material. Each man chewed on the fungus, keeping it in his mouth for a long time without swallowing. He sat motionless as the hallucinogen took effect, then rocked gently from side to side and without warning began to gesticulate convulsively, pupils widely dilated. He sang, danced and talked with someone he imagined was with him, but then, as the experience subsided, he urinated solemnly into an empty can labelled 'California Peaches'. The liquid was subsequently shared out and drunk. Among the Koryaks the fungus was only eaten by men, but in other cultures shamankas are known to have used it.

It may have been the source of the narcotic employed by the crazed bands of warriors recorded in Viking Scandinavia and known as the Berserks of Othin, men whose lives were dedicated to the war god. They were reputed to be immune from many of the laws which governed the rank and file, to have an almost sacred status and to fight in a state of ecstatic drug-induced frenzy, their origins possibly going back to Celtic times. Interestingly, in light of the Koryak story recalled above, they were also reputed to be capable of changing shape and taking on animal form, an ability which was generally considered the province of the shaman alone. Accounts of the conduct of Berserks almost invariably speak of individuals firstly entering a trancelike state of intoxication, and then being overcome by a ferocity and rage akin to that of a wild beast, responding neither to fear nor pain. While this behaviour was traditionally put down to the sacred powers of Othin, the sequence of moods would seem to tally with Jochelson's account of modern Koryaks entering a state of trance followed by extreme excitement under the influence of mycoatropine. In a person whose attitude was already aggressive, it is entirely probable that the effect of ingestion might be one of uncontrolled rage.

Much of the modern-day interest in *A. muscaria* was stimulated in the 1970s by the publication of a book entitled *The Sacred Mushroom and the Cross*, written by John Allegro. The book promoted an argument claiming that Christianity was no more than a cover for a mushroom-influenced fertility religion among initiates who consumed Fly Agaric. On close inspection Allegro was wholly unconvincing in his research, and he made claims which ignored the essential observation that *A. muscaria* is unknown in Syrio-Palestine, but the book became something of a cult study in the burgeoning dropout climate and it stimulated frequently dangerous experimentation.

Honey Fungus *(Armillaria mellea)*

Where and when

This large and distinctive mushroom grows, very commonly, in dense clusters on and around the stumps of broad-leaved and coniferous trees, the fruiting bodies emerging throughout the summer and autumn. At other times the presence of the fungus is revealed by the blackish-brown rhizomorphic cords of mycelium or vegetative body which run under the bark of an infected tree and give rise to the alternative common name of 'Bootlace Fungus'. Honey Fungus is a serious parasite and is responsible for the death of many trees and shrubs.

Appearance

The fruiting bodies are large and fleshy, tawny in colour, hence the name 'Honey Fungus', and finely scaly. The young cap is domed, then irregularly flattened, with the somewhat darker scales more densely arranged towards the centre, and the gills are at first white, becoming yellowish and then brown, tending to run down the stem. The stem is coloured similarly to the cap and possesses a cottony, yellowish ring towards the apex, the remnants of the incomplete or partial veil. The fungus has a somewhat acidic aroma, and while safely edible is also strongly flavoured and, for some people, rather indigestible.

Traditions and associations

Honey Fungus has been the indirect subject of mystery and magic since very early times, because it produces chemicals that possess a luminosity which causes the wood, through which its rhizomorphs penetrate, to glow or shine in the dark. This property has been virtually guaranteed to set the minds of the less scientifically informed buzzing with speculation! Frequently the light was attributed to glow-worms or other mysterious and even supernatural agencies.

The Elizabethan, Sir Francis Bacon, is credited with having made the first scientific study of luminosity in nature and it was he who established the link between the nocturnal luminance and wood that was both rotten and damp. It was left to J. F. Heller, however, in 1843, to identify the source of this particular type of luminescence as the mycelial strands of a fungus. A little more than 30 years later another botanist, Hartig, investigating the causes of wood rot, determined the species responsible for the phenomenon of the luminescence to be *Armillaria mellea* and established that it was the actively growing tips of the rhizomorphs that generated the light.

Bizarre tales abound concerning the uses to which luminous wood has been put including the insertion of pieces onto the helmets of trench soldiers during World War I to minimize the possibility of bumping into each other in the dark (from *Mushrooms and Toadstools* by J. Ramsbottom). In *Huckleberry Finn*, Mark Twain refers to luminous lumps of wood which he describes as 'foxfire' and there is the slightly distorted story of brightly glowing lumber in London timber yards during the last war causing consternation and being covered with tarpaulins. This, however, was probably less attributable to *Armillaria* than to phosphorous contamination from German incendiary bombs.

Probably the earliest historical record of luminous fungi is contained in the eighth-century *Beowulf* saga:

> *It is not far from here, if measured in miles, that a lake stands shadowed by trees stiff with hoar frost. A wood, firmly rooted, frowns over the water. There, night after night, a fearful wonder may be seen – fire on the water . . . that is not a pleasant place.*

In more southerly parts of Europe, a species of strongly luminous mushroom, *Omphalotus olearius*, grows around the bases of Olive trees. The species has been a subject of interest since Classical times when it was first described by Pliny but very recently, because of warmer climatic conditions, the species has become locally naturalized in parts of southern Britain, where it also uses Oak and Beech as its hosts.

Jew's Ear

(*Auricularia auricularia-judae*)

Where and when

A distinctively shaped fungus which grows predominantly on branches and trunks of Elder (*Sambucus nigra*), but also on other dead and dying wood including Beech (*Fagus*). The fruiting bodies can be found throughout the year but mainly in the autumn and winter months.

Appearance

A member of the group known as the Jelly Fungi, Jew's Ear emerges as a brown, ear-shaped, gelatinous fruiting body in small or large groups. The fruiting body is in an inverted cup-shape. The outer surface is tan-brown, with a purplish tinge when damp, and is covered with a fine down. The inner surface is shiny and smooth, but becomes wrinkled like an ear.

Traditions and associations

Any plant with physical characteristics that resemble human attributes instantly becomes fair game to be imbued with mystical connotations and the Jew's Ear Fungus, when fresh and fully grown, bears an uncanny resemblance to the human ear. Because of its striking shape and frequent appearance on Elder wood – a tree which has strong religious connotations with Judas Escariot, who is alleged to have hanged himself from an Elder – the fungus has earned the common tag of 'Jew's Ear' which is probably a corruption of 'Judas' Ear'. The Judas Escariot, story is wholly apocryphal and it is improbable that anyone ever hanged themselves from an Elder since the wood is too brittle to take the strain.

The fungus is edible and has been popular as the basis for a mushroom soup and for addition into casseroles. Like all the Jelly Fungi, it can be dried to a hard lump and successfully reconstituted by moistening in damp weather.

Magic Mushroom

(Psilocybe semilanceata)

Where and when

A very small, inconspicuous mushroom growing in scattered groups in short grass of pastures and gardens, preferring hilly locations and often associated with grazing sheep. The fruiting bodies appear from late summer to autumn and the species is infrequent, though perhaps locally more common.

Appearance

A small delicate mushroom with a distinctive yellowish pointed cap, drying a paler buff and feeling slightly sticky when wet. The young gills are clay-coloured but become dark or purplish-brown at maturity and the stem is proportionally long and slender, somewhat fibrous. It is coloured like the cap, although more pallid and sometimes with a bluish tinge towards the base. There is no evidence of a ring on the stem.

Traditions and associations

This is the species most conventionally referred to as the 'Magic Mushroom' because of its hallucinogenic properties and, as such, it is much sought after by interested parties when it first appears during the summer months. It is also known as 'Liberty Caps'. The chemicals it synthesizes include psilocin and psilocybin. Although the effects of ingesting the fungus were not unknown to past generations and it was probably in regular use by witches and wizards, it was not until 1958 that Albert Hoffman of LSD notoriety isolated the chemicals and isolated the cause of hallucination that was experienced by people who ate Magic Mushrooms.

The Magic Mushroom is primarily a 'product' of the hippy culture of the 1960s, but it has been sought after by devotees from all walks of life from bank managers to bus conductors, and there is an annual clandestine *Psilocybe* festival held each autumn at a discreet location in Wales. *P. semilanceata* is closely related to an American species, *P. mexicana,* which is of enormous traditional importance and social consequence throughout large parts of Central and South America, where it is frequently employed by elderly wise women, as it must have been in Europe during much of the Medieval period, to dispense village magic and cure.

Symptoms of ingestion of either species include heightened perception both of sounds and visual images, and feelings which may be euphoric or of nightmarish proportions depending on the prior mood of the person. The symptoms commence after about 20 minutes and may continue for many hours, becoming more intense before waning. According to the Poisons Information Service based in London, the 'flashbacks' can occur for several days afterwards.

Stinkhorn *(Phallus impudicus)*

Where and when

The fruiting bodies are a common sight in woodlands from early summer to autumn, usually in association with rotten and buried wood. This bizarrely shaped fungus emerges through the soil from a partly submerged 'egg' and expands upwards with great speed overnight.

Appearance

A phallic-shaped structure which arises from the white rubbery 'egg' as a result of the rapid upward expansion of a white, spongy, stem-like receptacle, 10–25 cm (4–10 in) tall. At the top of this 'stalk' is mounted a pitted conical head, up to 4 cm (1½ in) in diameter, and carrying the spore mass. The spores are embedded in an olive-green slime which gives off a foul and very penetrating smell, similar to that of decomposing meat, which attracts flies. The spores are thus dispersed by the passage of insects. The smell is so distinctive that often a Stinkhorn concealed in undergrowth many metres away can be tracked down purely by following the aroma.

Traditions and associations

Many fungi bear similarity to a phallus while in their young state, but none so strikingly as the Stinkhorn and its diminutive cousin the Dog Stinkhorn (*Mutinus caninus*). Stinkhorn is a rather more polite alternative, coined by the Victorians, to the more pithy translation of the Latin, 'brazen phallus'. Earlier textbooks were less coy. Gerard, in his *Herball* of 1638, entitled it the 'Pricke Mushrom' and added the almost superfluous Latin observation of Clusius, *Fungus Virilis Penis effigie*. Gerard also copied the illustration of the Roman writer but, in order not to offend the sensitivities of his readers, the drawing was reproduced upside down.

Predictably, perhaps, the fungus has long been regarded as an aphrodisiac and in some countries the burnt and powdered fruiting body is applied to the genitalia of infertile women as a quack treatment. One of the most amusing anecdotes reflecting Victorian prudishness, and the view that such objects should not be seen by young unmarried women, comes from a more general observation of *P. impudicus* made concerning Charles Darwin's eldest daughter, Etty:

> *Armed with a basket and a pointed stick, and wearing a special hunting cloak and gloves, she [Etty] would sniff her way around the wood, pausing here and there, her nostrils twitching when she caught a whiff of her prey. Then with a deadly pounce she would fall upon her victim and poke his putrid carcass into her basket. At the end of the day's sport the catch was brought back and burnt in the deepest secrecy of the drawing room fire with the door locked – because of the morals of the maids.*
>
> (Taken from *Period Piece* by Gwen Raverat)

Various notions have arisen over the strange 'eggs' from which the stinkhorns arise, including the possibility, held in Austrian country districts, that they spawn evil spirits or devils. They are also widely assumed to have been left behind where deer have rutted.

Witches' Butter

(Exidia glandulosa)

Where and when

Arising on the dead and rotting branches, and on the wound tissue of the living wood, among a variety of hardwood trees, the fruiting bodies appear infrequently, and although they occur mainly in late summer and autumn they are visible throughout the year.

Appearance

A contorted, blackish-brown gelatinous mass which occurs in both small and larger groups up to 30 cm (1 ft) in diameter and which is made up of wrinkled discs that become folded and somewhat brainlike. Like other Jelly Fungi belonging to the mycological group known as the Heterobasidiomycetes, Witches' Butter has the ability to withstand considerable desiccation, reviving fully with the onset of damp weather.

Traditions and associations

Because of its colour and sinister, brain-like appearance, coupled with a gelatinous and rather slimy texture, this fungus has been traditionally associated with witches. It was supposedly deposited by them as a by-product of the illicit milking of cows in the dead of night.

Further Reading

Baker, M. *The Folklore of Plants*, Shire Publications, 1971.

Bentham and Hooker *Handbook of the British Flora*, Reeve, 1954.

Ellis Davidson, H. R. *Gods and Myths of Northern Europe*, Penguin, 1964.

Findlay, W. P. K. *Fungi - Folklore, Fiction and Fact*, Richmond Publishing, 1982.

Frazer, J. G. *The Golden Bough*, Macmillan, 1983.

Graves, R. *The White Goddess*, Faber and Faber, 1988.

Grimal, P. *Dictionary of Classical Mythology*, Penguin, 1991.

Hollander, Lee M. *The Poetic Edda*, Texas University Press, 1962.

Homer *The Odyssey*, Oxford University Press (W. Shewring translation), 1980.

Jordan, M. *The Encyclopedia of Gods*, Kyle Cathie, 1992.

Jordan, M. *The Encyclopedia of Fungi of Great Britain and Europe*, David and Charles, 1995.

Keble Martin, W. *The New Concise British Flora*, BCA, 1982.

McClintock and Fitter *Wild Flowers*, Collins, 1965.

Skinner, C. M. *Myths and Legends of Flowers, Trees, Fruits and Plants*, Philadelphia, 1911.

Sturluson, S. *Edda*, Dent, (A. Faulkes translation), 1987.

Thistleton-Dyer, T. F. *The Folklore of Plants*, London, 1889.

Vickery, R. *A Dictionary of Plant Lore*, Oxford University Press, 1995.

Index